Creation Speaks for Itself

# ANiMALS
## Could Talk

# DR. WERNER GITT

Master
Books®
A Division of New Leaf Publishing Group
www.masterbooks.net

Creation
Speaks for
Itself

# If ANiMALS Could Talk

## DR. WERNER GITT

First Master Books printing: January 2006
Fourth printing: October 2014

Master Books®, P.O. Box 726, Green Forest, AR 72638.
Master Books® is a division of the New Leaf Publishing Group, Inc.

Translation to English: Allan Collister and Mark Garvey

ISBN-13: 978-0-89051-460-3
Library of Congress Number: 2005934370

Cover by Left Coast Design, Portland, OR

All Scripture is from the King James Version of the Bible unless otherwise noted.

Please consider requesting that a copy of this volume be purchased by your local library system.

**Printed in the United States of America**

Please visit our website for other great titles:
www.masterbooks.net

For information regarding author interviews, please contact the publicity department at (870) 438-5288.

Master
Books®
A Division of New Leaf Publishing Group
www.masterbooks.net

# CONTENTS

# PREFACE

Animals have very efficient communication systems, which they use to converse with one another. Nevertheless, they are not able to speak to us in human language. So we have projected ourselves into them, and we have made ourselves their "mouthpieces." That's the reason for the title of the book: *If Animals Could Talk*. If animals could tell us about themselves, using our scientific knowledge, if they could tell us about the way they live, the special way they are made and many details about their individual design — what they would say would be unique praise to the Creator. We have therefore chosen certain animals and would like to speak for them in order to show something of the great Creator himself: the rich treasure of His ideas, His joy in creating, His love for beauty in form and color, His painstaking care and finally, His love for humankind and His desire to save us through Jesus Christ.

The book is written in a way that would present each individual animal of a particular species as an imaginary dialogue partner for the reader. Each animal deals with questions that might arise, and answers them in this hypothetical conversation. Through this method, the material is presented in a narrative form and, we hope, in a lively and entertaining way. We have not tried to skip difficult topics, but have tried to deal with them in the same narrative way, and make them accessible. We have often taken examples from everyday experience to clarify detail, or to show it in its proper context. We think that this method makes statistical information more comprehensive.

*Literary Genre:* This book is neither a dry book of facts, nor a scientific treatment, but rather an engaging "dialogue" between certain creatures and us humans. While at a superficial glance, these stories might appear to be fairy tales or fables, such an evaluation would be essentially false. Rather, we are dealing with a special literary genre which deals responsibly with factual matter, but as a stylistic tool, has animals speak for themselves, and thus describe the works of God and praise their Creator.

> But ask now the beasts,
> and they shall teach thee;
> and the fowls of the air,
> and they shall tell thee:
> Or speak to the earth,
> and it shall teach thee:
> and the fishes of the sea
> shall declare unto thee.
> Who knoweth not in all these
> that the hand of the LORD
> hath wrought this?
> In whose hand
> is the soul of every living thing,
> and the breath of all mankind
> (Job 12:7–10; KJV).

Through this book we are also making a stand for the protection of the animal kingdom. Mankind has received a vocation from God:

> . . . have dominion over the fish of the sea, and over the fowl of the air, and over every living thing that moveth upon the earth (Gen. 1:28).

We have therefore been appointed as administrators over the animals. We will eventually be called on by Him to give an account of ourselves in this capacity. For this reason, cruelty to animals and the extermination of complete animal groups, which is often purely based on profit grounds (e.g., whales), can only be condemned.

*Contents:* Out of the great diversity of the animal kingdom, with more than a million different species, we have selected only a very small sample. Despite this limitation, they are all real animals, on the earth, in the earth, in the water, or in the air, that talk to us. The one exception to this is where one tiny part of the human anatomy talks to us about God's construction principles. The facts presented have been scientifically confirmed, even if they are presented in a non-scientific form, due to the narrative style we have chosen. In order not to disturb the flow of reading by constantly referring to source literature, we have generally omitted footnotes.

*Circle of Readers:* We have not been writing for a specific type of reader, in terms of age, education, or profession. Rather, we want to be accessible to everybody — young and old, laymen as well as experts. Furthermore, the conversations will be valuable, whether the reader believes in God or doubts His existence. Actually, we have been writing more for the "seeker" than for anybody else. We have smoothed the way for such a person, without biblical preparation or knowledge, so that he or she can come to know the Creator personally.

*Acknowledgments:* We are grateful to Allan Collister and Mark Garvey who were able to devote their valuable time to the translation of this book. A special note of appreciation is due to Sarah J. Curtius, Colette Drescher, and Thomas Ruchatz who edited the translation.

— Werner Gitt and Karl-Heinz Vanheiden

# PREFACE TO THE
# SECOND ENGLISH EDITION

This book first appeared in Germany in 1990. It is now in its tenth edition, with 300,000 copies in circulation. In the meantime, translations have appeared in a number of languages — e.g., Bulgarian, Chinese, Croatian, Czech, French, Hungarian, Polish, Romanian, and Russian. We are delighted to know that it has won so many friends at home and abroad. Among them have been those who have made the breakthrough in their thinking from evolution to creation, and have also found the Creator as their personal Lord.

The authors are also delighted that this book is now appearing for the second time in the English language. The first edition was thoroughly checked from a technical as well as linguistic standpoint and improved in several places. This effort was undertaken by the scientist/writer Russell Grigg (M.Sc), who works for the world-renowned organization for creation science/research, Answers in Genesis, in Brisbane, Australia. Russell is well known to the readers of their colorful magazine *Creation ex Nihilo* (print run > 50,000, with subscribers in over 120 countries) for his thought-provoking articles. We want to thank him most sincerely for this careful reworking of the English text.

# CHAPTER 1

# SPEAKING OF BIRDBRAIN!

## *The Field Sparrow*

It is true that there are quite a lot of us. Our song is loud, and not very appealing. People think we eat their crops. Even our humble appearance doesn't earn us any admirers. But still, if you take the trouble to pay attention to a cheeky sparrow, you'll find it worthwhile. I promise you that.

You think you won't find anything special about me, do you? Well, there are just as many of us as there are of you. You think that just because there are lots of something, that makes it irrelevant? Then you would have to be pretty unimportant yourself! Oh, excuse me, I was being really impertinent.

Actually, I am a well-mannered field sparrow. I wouldn't want you to confuse me with my cousin, the fat and cheeky house sparrow. You can recognize me by my grey breast and the black patch on my wing, so you can easily tell us apart. As my name suggests, I tend to keep away from your houses.

## BORN TO FLY

My Creator designed me first and foremost as a flier. For that reason, every last part of my body is designed for flight. I can't figure out how some people have the nerve to say that we descended from reptiles. Just imagine! Dinosaurs are supposed to be our closest relatives! Nobody can make me believe that the first sparrow lived more than 50 million years ago. It seems to me that the fairy-tale character of this whole theory is camouflaged by the huge number of years, but let's leave that theory aside and concentrate on the facts. Then you can judge for yourself.

My body is made of the lightest material imaginable. Almost all my bones are hollow. This means they can take to the air. They are very light, but remain stable. A distant relative of mine, the albatross, has bones that have a combined weight of only 4.2 to 5.3 ounces (120 to 150 gm), even though he is 39 inches (1 m) long, and has a wingspan of almost 10 feet (3 m). The weight of his feathers exceeds the weight of his bones!

If our bones were full of marrow, like those of the reptiles, we could never fly. Besides that, our pelvis is attached to our spine, which is not the case with reptiles. That's the only way that our skeleton has the strength and elasticity that is essential for flying.

## A REMARKABLE HOLE

The small hole in the linkage of my upper arm bone seems pretty remarkable to me. This is not a defect. The ligament which connects the breast muscle with the upper side of the shoulder joint goes through this hole. Without this, I wouldn't be able to lift my wing, let alone fly. If I descended from reptiles, then I would have to ask myself, who drilled that hole in the glenoid cavity? Who threaded the ligament through the hole? You will look long and hard before you find a hole like that in a crocodile or in a dinosaur.

## BE STRONG, MY HEART!

Squawk! Help, a sparrow hawk! Squawk! Where can I hide? Help! Oh, I got away again! That was a close one! Now he's gone again. Did you know, the sparrow hawk is our worst enemy? With his long claws he can even grab us out of the thickest bush, if we don't watch out. We've got a whole crowd of enemies: crows, magpies, cats, and humans. They don't even leave us alone at night. The owls grab us from the branches where we sleep. I remember one time when a horrible screech owl broke into our nest in the middle of the night, tore my husband out and mercilessly ripped him apart from head to toe. It was terrible!

Nevertheless, I know that my Creator cares for me. In the Bible it says that God doesn't forget a single sparrow. It must be even better for you, as you're much more valuable to Him than I am. He has even numbered the hairs on your head. Yes, God obviously cares for you humans in a special way.

You know, my Creator gave me an exceptionally strong heart. It is one of the most efficient hearts there are. At the moment, while talking to you, it's beating more than seven times a second, or 460 times a minute. Just now, when I was fleeing from the sparrow hawk, my pulse went up to 760! It has to beat that fast to enable me to fly.

## A SUPER TOOL

Yes, look at me more closely. Do you see my beak? Not very remarkable from the outside, right? But it is a miraculous tool which my Creator gave me: super-light, and yet capable of the hardest tasks. Somebody figured out that the tearing length of the horn of my beak is about 20 miles (31 km). That means, if you made a wire of this material, and could fasten it somewhere, then the wire would only tear as a result of its own weight when it was longer than 50 miles. The material that you humans use for aircraft construction has a tearing length of just 11 miles (18 km).

## A Look Through the Telescope

Did you know that my entire skull is lighter than both my eyeballs? That doesn't mean that you have to make nasty remarks about my bird brain. My eyes are far better than yours are. We birds have seven to eight times more visual cells per unit of surface area than you. That way we have an image in our brains that is much sharper than yours. For example, if you wanted to see an object as clearly as a buzzard does, you would have to use a (8 × 30) telescope. I admit, my eyes are not quite so sharp, but I'm still sure that they are much better than yours. A biologist wrote that my eye is a miracle of construction, function, and efficiency. It is one of the most perfect optical organs in the vertebrate world. It has to be, because even when we are flying at our fastest we can't afford to miss any important detail.

Besides our sharp eyes, God also gave us a very flexible neck. It is so flexible that we can reach every part of our body with our beak. Do you think this is just a coincidence? You try touching your forehead to your knee while standing. Oh, so you can do it, can you? No, there's no need to do it now. If you really can do it, you'll probably hear your bones cracking. For me, this flexibility is a matter of life and death.

## Digestion Is a Must

What did you say? God made me so that eating's all I'm good for? My Creator and I won't accept such an insult. Do you actually have any idea what I eat? Yes, that's what I thought. He who knows the least shouts the loudest! Oh, excuse me. I'm being cheeky again, but you weren't so polite yourself!

In China, my relatives almost became extinct, because certain people thought that we field sparrows ate too much rice and millet. As they went through the process of almost exterminating our race, they realized that vermin were taking over their fields. Their losses were even higher than before. Our actual diet consists of small animals that you regard as pests, but which we treasure as delicacies: cockchafers, flying ants, larvae of the green oak leaf roller, apple blossom weevils, leaf lice, etc.

Speaking of eating, have you any idea as to how our digestion functions? Actually, it's quite an interesting topic. As you know, everything about me is geared to flight. Since I eat so much protein, I can get by with a very short intestine, but I need very powerful digestive juices. My Creator didn't want to weigh me down with useless by-products of digestion. So I drop the stuff out as fast as I can — often while I'm flying. I know that I sometimes manage to "decorate" your clothing that way. I'm terribly sorry!

My builder did something very ingenious when He made me. He omitted my bladder completely. That way, He was able to make my body more slender at the rear, which helps for streamlining, and keeps my weight down. Eighty percent of my urine consists of uric acid, which crystallizes into a white paste at the very end of my intestine. Isn't that a nifty solution? Furthermore, almost all the water necessary for the excretory process is recovered into the organism. So I don't need to "tank up" on water too often.

## CATAPULT AND JACKKNIFE

Can you be patient a little longer? Take another look at my feet! They don't look like much, but they're really a fairly refined design. It's true: all you can see are my feet and toes. The rest of my leg, calf, knee, and thigh, are all hidden in my body. And if you think I'm standing upright, I'm actually crouching with my knees bent. For you, this position might be uncomfortable, but not for me. If I suddenly straighten my knees out, my muscles launch me upward like a catapult, and I immediately put my wings into action. During flight, I simply retract my "landing gear" up under my feathers, and extend it again when I'm ready to land. Here again, its high elasticity is most helpful.

Have you ever stopped to wonder how I can sit for hours at a time on a twig, and can even sleep in this position? My Creator made that possible by means of a very special mechanism, which automatically wraps my toes around the branch so that they hold on tight. A whole bundle of ligaments are connected from the toes to the thigh muscle. If I sit on a branch, these ligaments are tightened simply by my body weight, and they pull the toes together. Besides that, at a certain place on the ligaments there are tiny hooks. When I sit down, these hooks fasten themselves firmly into tiny teeth — again, this is no accident — exactly in the right place in the coating of the ligament sheath. So the ligaments remain under tension, without any effort on my part, and I don't fall from the tree.

For long-legged birds like storks and herons, who have to stand for long periods of time, the design is a little bit different. They have been given a special knee joint that engages like a jackknife. So they have no problem standing for hours.

## WHY WE LAY EGGS

Why do you think we birds don't give birth to our young like mammals do? You don't know? Well, just imagine what it would be like for a pregnant bird to fly, with her large belly. How would I feed myself for that period of time, if I were only able to walk around on the ground? The whole egg-laying system is one of our Creator's patent ideas. It keeps me from being weighed down while flying. I lay my eggs one after another, at intervals of no more than 24 hours on average. That means that the egg-laying is finished quickly, and the eggs can all be incubated simultaneously. In this way, we birds can bring several young into the world at the same time.

## THE ART OF BROODING

You probably think that this is one of the most boring occupations possible. That's just because you have no idea of how difficult it really is. Do you really think we just set ourselves down on the eggs, and wait until the young are hatched? Have you any idea how sensitive our chicks really are? We have to provide just the right temperature, exactly the right level of moisture, and even an undisturbed gas exchange. If these conditions weren't right, our chicks would die before they were even born.

But our Creator had an ingenious idea, and it works like this: Even before I begin to lay eggs, the downy feathers on my belly fall out at two or three strategic locations. The exposed skin becomes noticeably thicker than before. The blood vessels increase sevenfold in number, and are about five times as thick as before. At the same time, lots of fluids accumulate in the cells of these "brooding spots." What is all this? As soon as a brooding spot touches the egg, the egg temperature is reported to my middle brain. From there, the temperature is either directly controlled, or it is made clear to me that I need to move my body from the eggs so they can get some air, or that it's time to get back to my "brooding post."

How this reporting into the middle brain takes place, and how I pass on information to my unhatched chicks through this brooding spot, remains a complete mystery to your scientists. Even so, many of them quite casually suggest that this process gradually evolved. I'd just like to ask these people, how my ancestors ever succeeded in hatching their young, if they weren't able to tell whether their eggs were too hot or too cold?

Oh, there's so much more I could tell you, about my lung system, the miracle of flight, the super-construction of my feathers, my navigation system. . . . But I'll leave that all to my colleague, the swallow, who is much more of an expert in such matters.

Just tell me this: Do you still believe that I'm a descendent of some kind of creeping animal? No, my Creator is neither "coincidence" nor "millions of years." My Creator is the One who spoke the word on the fifth day, that birds were to fly over the earth. He is the One who created all of us after our kinds. He is the One who blessed us, and delights in us. I am a miraculous work of His hands. You, too! We really ought to praise Him together!

# CHAPTER 2

# FOUNTAINS FOR FINGERPRINTS

## *The Whales*

We whales are living superlatives. Did you realize that? I'd like to tell you about the wonderful capabilities and special characteristics which the Creator gave us, that you won't find anywhere else in the animal kingdom. For instance, did you know:

– that there are whales that can eat while moving at a speed of 6 mph (10 km/h), can travel long distances at 22 mph (35 km/h), and — if they have to — can even get up to 40 mph (65 km/h)?

- that there are whales that carry out annual migrations of 6,200 miles (10,000 km), just like certain migrating birds?

- that whales can compose music?

- that there are whales that can blow a spout of water 50 feet (15 m) high, just by breathing out?

- that there are whales, that at 9,800 feet (3,000 m), hold the deep-diving record?

- that certain whales can generate more than 850 kilowatts of power (your cars only have about one-tenth as much)?

- that some whales have a lung volume of more than 800 gallons (3,000 l)? You humans have a lung capacity of just over 1 gallon (4 l), or at most, 1.8 gallons (7 l).

- that there are whales that produce milk with a world record butter-fat content of 42%? (Your mothers' milk has a butter-fat content of 4.4%, about one-tenth of a whale's value.)

- that certain whales have tongues so heavy that they weigh as much as two fully grown horses?

- that there are whales with aortas 20 inches (50 cm) in diameter, which is about the size of a water main?

Why am I telling you all this? It's really not that important to us to have a place in your *Guinness Book of Records*. We care about something more important: Have you ever noticed, when you read the creation accounts in Genesis, that we are the only animals that are actually mentioned by name? "And God created great whales, and every living creature that moveth, which the waters brought forth abundantly, after their kind" (Gen. 1:21).

How come? Is it because God went to great lengths to create us? Did He take special pleasure in us? Granted, we can't figure out His deeper motives, but just think! We found special significance as a hidden testimony to the resurrection of Jesus from the dead. When the critics of the Lord Jesus once demanded a sign from Him, He pointed to the story of Jonah: "For as Jonah was three days and three nights in the belly of a huge fish [Greek: *cetos* not *ichthys*, the word usually used for fish], so the Son of Man will be three days and three nights in the heart of the earth" (Matt. 12:40). In that way, the Lord Jesus pointed to His own resurrection. Have you ever considered what kind of sea animal has a stomach big enough to hold a human being? If you check, you'll find that only our species fits the bill. Since we have been so honored in the order of creation, we consider ourselves witnesses to the resurrection of Jesus, and more than that, to the grace of God. Let me give you some more details about our life, and some amazing facts about our species, so that you can draw your own conclusions.

Your scientists did not catalogue us according to the variations in our size, lifestyles, methods of capturing food, or our habitat in the ocean. Rather, they have concentrated on the variations in our teeth, and categorized us into two different groups (zoological suborders): Mystacocete (baleen whales) and Odontocete (toothed whales). **Baleen whales** may be grouped into three distinct families: *Right whales* (Greenland right whale, northern right whale, North Pacific right whale, southern right whale, pygmy right whale), *grey whales,* and *rorquals* (blue whale, dwarf blue whale, fin whale, Bryde's whale, humpback whale). The sub-species of **toothed whales** is formed by the families: *sperm whale, beaked* (black whale, northern bottlenose), *white whales, porpoises,* and *dolphins.*

Our habitat is the ocean, but remember, whales are flesh mammals, not fish! We give birth to our young. It is true that the Ree Barsch does this too, but naturally, there is not a single fish that can nurse its young. Even though we live exclusively in the sea, we are actually mammals, and so we also breathe through our lungs. We keep our body temperature fixed at 97.7 degrees Fahrenheit (36.5°C) — regardless of whether we are in the icy waters of Antarctica or in the warm waters of Bermuda. As you can imagine, these conditions cause a whole group of special problems, but the Creator solved these problems for us in a wonderful way.

## OUR BIRTH AND INFANCY

We whales have the same partner throughout our lifetime. Our infants are born and bred in the water. A mature female gives birth to one offspring about every two years. Pregnancy does not last as long as you might imagine for an animal of our size: only 10 to 12 months. I'm a Sperm Whale — I actually have a pregnancy of 16 months. Compared with the rhinoceros (18 months) and the elephant (22 months), we are quick. When the time for the birth approaches, we look for a place that is secure from storms. Our most important nurseries are the lagoons of Baja California for the grey whale, the Sea of Cortez for the blue whale, the coasts of the Hawaiian Island of Maui or certain islands of the Bahamas for the humpback whale, and the area around the Azores, the Galapagos Islands, or Sri Lanka for me. Seals go on the land to give birth to their young, but we do it all in the water. Just imagine what it would be like if our babies were born head-first: if the birth took any time at all, they would be forced to take their first breath while their head was still under water, and they would drown. But our Creator had thought this all out, and He arranged things for us differently than for any other mammal: All whales are born in the breech position, i.e., the baby whale appears tail first. In this way, the infant remains connected to its life support system (its mother's umbilical cord) for as long as possible.

There aren't any sheltering caves or other places of refuge for the newborn to be hidden in, so this security is provided by the helpful care of the other members of the group, as well as by the loving attention of the mother. Even as babies, we can't be overlooked. The infant blue whale is 26 feet (8 m) long at birth, and weighs 8 tons. That's 4,400 pounds (2,000 kg) more than an adult elephant weighs. To come up to its length at birth, at least three elephants would have to be lined up in a row. Other whale babies aren't that much smaller than the blue whale:

- Greenland whale: 20 feet (6 m), 6 tons
- Northern right whale: 16.4 feet (5 m), 5 tons
- Humpback whale: 15 feet (4.5 m), 2.5 tons
- Grey whale: 15 feet (4.5 m), 1.5 tons

Nursing under water has its problems, too. So the Creator provided wonderful equipment for us. The mother squirts her milk directly from her teat into the mouth of her infant. This takes place with such pressure that it would cause a milk fountain on the surface 6-1/2 feet (2 m) high. The breast lies in a pocket-shaped fold, so that it doesn't disturb her streamlining. The whale baby has to grow fast, in order to be strong enough for the rapidly approaching return migration into the polar waters. The milk it drinks is the most nutritious milk that exists; it has 42% butterfat content, and 12% protein (compared with human milk: 4.4% butterfat, and 1% protein). It is very thick and creamy. This calorie bomb, which is 100 times as nutritious as an adult human would require, causes the baby whale to grow at a breathtaking rate. While a human infant takes 180 days to double its birth weight, a whale baby takes a lot less time. During the seven months before it is weaned, a baby blue whale drinks 200 pounds (90 kg) of milk daily. Every 24 hours, it grows from 1.2 to 1.6 inches (3 to 4 cm), and increases in weight by about 175 pounds (80 kg). That makes 7.3 pounds (3.3 kg) per hour! Some 18 to 19 tons of this extremely dense milk cause the baby whale to grow 17 tons during the entire time it is nursing. Isn't that a sensational degree of efficiency?

Oh, there goes my relative, the blue whale. He'll be only too glad to tell you more about himself. If you like the unusual, you'll want to pay special attention to him.

## THE BLUE WHALE — GIANT OF THE ANIMAL KINGDOM

I am the largest of all 80 types of whale. My body weight is many times more than that of the largest dinosaurs. In fact, I am the largest animal that has ever existed on earth. To match my weight, you would have to bring together a herd of 28 elephants, or 170 oxen. If you wanted to match my weight with human beings, you would need 2,000 people. If you wanted to compare me with the smallest animal — Suvi's pygmy shrew — I weigh 70 million times more than he does! I can even dazzle you with my length. At 108 feet (33 m) long, I am the longest creature of all. I would easily be longer than a column of four buses. If you like details, I can give you a few. My skeleton weighs 22 tons, and my body fat 25 tons. In addition, my flesh weighs 50 tons. My tongue alone is as heavy as an elephant. My heart is 47 inches (1.2 m) in diameter, and weighs as much as a horse. It pumps a grand total of 2,600 gallons (10,000 l) of blood through my system. My aorta is a tube with a diameter of more than 20 inches (50 cm). My liver weighs a ton, and my stomach can hold the same weight in food. My kidney is approximately the same weight as an ox.

You think I'm just a shapeless mountain of meat and fat? Don't jump to conclusions! I can effortlessly dive to a depth of 660 feet (200 m), and it's no problem for me to keep my course even in strong currents. If I swim on the surface, I can move at a speed of 17.3 mph (28 km/h). To do that, I have to generate 1,175 horsepower, which, in turn, requires 20,000 liters of oxygen per minute (5,300 gallons). If I swim at the same speed under water, it only takes me 168 horsepower, and that means only 3,000 liters of oxygen (800 gallons). My lungs hold a volume of 3,000 liters; that's enough air to fill 750 balloons.

*Fluke High Performance Engine:* You might well be fascinated with my gigantic whale-tail, which is known as the fluke. In contrast to those of fish, whose tails are vertical, ours are horizontal. Your evolutionist scientists have suggested that my tail is a regressive development of the hind legs of our supposed land-dwelling ancestors. The real reason is different: The Creator designed our tail to be horizontal, because in terms of fluid dynamics it is much more practical for us with our constant diving and surfacing, than a vertical tail could ever be. If I want to surface, I just drive my fluke downward. If I want to dive, I force it the other way. The fluke forms a surface of 108 square feet (10 square m). It has been made in a most complicated way, so that it can fulfill its purpose without any problems. I use my fluke to propel myself, but I also use it to stabilize and steer myself. To propel myself, I drive my fluke in a sort of turning motion, the axis of which would form an extension of my spine. It's true that I can't move it in a full circle like a ship's screw, but I always turn it to the same extent in one direction, and then in the other. The working principle is pretty much the same. In my worldwide migrations, I easily maintain a long-term speed of 22 mph (35 km/h). Sometimes I accelerate my gigantic body to a speed of 31 mph (50 km/h). My body shape and skin is so formed that I am able to propel myself with the highest possible degree of efficiency. If your fluid dynamics engineers could make a model of our body, and equip it with the same power engine that our bodies possess, we would still swim significantly faster than their model. The Creator provided us with a special skin, which helps us to save energy. It enables us to reduce turbulence in the water streaming over our bodies, and transform it into laminar flow with reduced resistance. This occurs, among other things, through the extra smoothness of our skin. This captures a portion of the turbulent energy of the water, and achieves a damping effect of the vortices near the surface of our skin over our entire body.

Doesn't the Creator perfect some new miracle in each one of our species? Each one of us originates in just as microscopically small an egg as that of a mouse, or of a human.

After reporting on the blue whale, I'd now like to introduce:

## THE SPERM WHALE — RECORD HOLDER
## IN DEEP SEA DIVING

Deep dives of 1,150 feet (350 m) and more are no problem for bottlenose dolphins and rorquals. The beaked whale can dive to a depth of 1,640 feet (500 m), and the weddell seal can even reach 1,970 feet (600 m). Have you noticed how we whales are all clearly different from one another? With a length of 49–59 feet (15–18 m), and a weight of 60 tons (55,000 kg), I am the largest representative of the toothed whales. I only have teeth in my lower jaw; in my upper jaw, there are about 40 holes. The teeth in my lower jaw are about 7.8 inches (20 cm) long, barrel shaped, and exactly the same size. They fit exactly into the holes in my upper jaw.

However, my most important trait is my ability to dive to extreme depths. Dives of 3,280 feet (1,000 m) are no problem for me. Sometimes, I even dive to a depth of 9,845 feet (3,000 m). What is wrong? Oh, you're trying to work it all out! Don't you trust your results? It's really true! With every 33 feet (10 m) of increased depth that I dive, there is an additional pressure on my body of one atmosphere. Since I dive at a vertical speed of 4.3 to 5 mph (7 to 8 km/h), I even have to cope with an extra pressure of more than one atmosphere in my own body because of my length. At 3,280 feet (1,000 m), the pressure climbs to 101 atmospheres. That amounts to 223 pounds (101 kg) of pressure on every square centimeter (less than ½ inch) of my body. That's the same as if you had to bear the weight of a heavyweight boxer on your fingernail. But you're wondering about something else — how do I deal with diver's disease — "the bends"?[1] Don't worry; there's no danger. My master builder

---

1. The bends (decompression sickness) in humans: Water pressure increases uniformly with increasing depth. With decreasing pressure as the diver ascends, the air, carried from the lungs by the blood, is released and forms air bubbles in the blood. If the diver should surface too quickly, i.e., if the water pressure is rapidly decreased, then the released air — especially the nitrogen — does not have enough time to

figured out all these details, and equipped me accordingly. I'd like to tell you about it.

You probably think that the deep-diving whales (sperm whales, northern bottle-nose whales, rorquals), who can effortlessly spend an hour and a half under water, must have enormous lungs. In fact, the opposite is true. Compared with our body size, we have remarkably small lungs. Humans have a lung volume about 1.76% of body size. Elephants' lungs are 2.55% of body volume. Our corresponding values are much smaller: for me, 0.91%; blue whales, 0.73%; and northern right whales, 0.65%. We, however, by means of a whole array of mechanisms, utilize our lung capacity much more intensively than land mammals do. For instance, we have substantially smaller air chambers. Our blood has a 50% higher level of hemoglobin than human blood. Thus, we have a much higher capability to transport oxygen. You utilize only 10 to 20% of your breathed air for energy, but we utilize between 80 and 90%. You see, when we take a breath, it is as effective as if you were to breathe eight times.

We can prepare for diving differently from any other mammal. Part of that preparation comes from a special capability that the Creator gave us, which enables our muscles to store oxygen in a unique way. Behind that capability are unique organic construction methods and special physiological equipment. Now you can just imagine how I prepare myself for a deep dive. Without haste or stress, I go through a ten-minute-long breathing phase, and fill all my oxygen storage capacity. It is easy to remember: for every minute of diving, I prepare myself with one breath. If I take 60 breaths, I can spend about three quarters of an hour at 3,280 feet (1000 m) depth. It takes me about 15 minutes to descend and ascend, which easily leaves me 45 minutes at depth.

---

get back into the blood and return to the lungs. Just like suddenly opening a champagne bottle, many gas bubbles merge, stopping up blood vessels and causing deadly embolism or clots. To inhibit this sickness, the diver has to surface gradually, and revert to normal pressure in special decompression chambers.

There is another important difference you should know about: when you dive, 34% of your oxygen comes from your lungs, 41% from your blood, and 25% from your muscles and tissues. For us, it is fundamentally different: only 9% comes from our lungs and 41% from our blood, leaving 50% from muscles and tissues. Underwater, therefore, our lungs only play a subordinate role.

Now you probably ask: How do our lungs respond if they are exposed to such crushing pressures? Don't our lungs just fall in on themselves like a wet sack and collapse? In all land mammals, it is only the windpipe and the large bronchial tubes that are equipped with supporting rings, so that they are able to remain open while inhaling. You have seen this kind of reinforcement on the suction hose of your vacuum cleaner. For whales, the Creator provided this kind of reinforcement into the smallest branches of the bronchial tree. In this way, our air passages simply cannot be collapsed. In addition, this construction allows for quick ventilation of our lungs.

In order to give us the longest possible diving time, the Creator also gave us an incomparable energy conservation program. During a dive, our heart beats only half as rapidly as it does on the surface. Nonessential regions or parts of our body can be more or less shut off from the circulation system. The blood stream is redirected and regulated by a system of vein closure muscles. The whole thing works somewhat like a network of one-way streets. During the diving phase, only important organs, such as the brain, the heart, and the tail structure, are provided with oxygen. An essential part of our diving technique is the so-called miracle network *(rete mirabile)*, which the Creator built only into us whales. Your scientists have not yet figured out all of its complex functions, but the miracle network plays a central role in oxygen management and pressure equalization.

What's this masterful diving equipment for? Why do I dive to the bottom, where there's no sunshine — into the eternal night and the darkest depths? Some people say that I am the all-time champion when it comes to eating — that I'll eat anything.

To be honest, squid are my favorite dish, and they are only to be found at great depths. I eat small squid by the thousands. Your whalers once counted 28,000 of them in the stomach of one of our dead colleagues. I even eat the larger squid by the dozen. To tell the truth, the ocean floor is the only place you can find the greatest delicacy of all: giant octopus. There are lots of tall tales about these animals, which can be as big as 26 feet (8 m), with tentacles as long as 49 feet (15 m). I have eaten whoppers like that whole. Usually there is a real "battle of the giants" before he lands up in my stomach. With my fine locating system, I can find my prey without fail. I send out little clicks, and listen for the echoes. Despite the deepest darkness, my sonar system gives me precise information about the number and size of my prey.

## OUR NOSE — NOT ON THE FACE, BUT ON TOP OF THE HEAD

In contrast with all land mammals, our noses are not fixed in the middle of the face, but on the upper surface of the head. The Creator did it this way so that when we are swimming horizontally our noses are on the highest part of our bodies. Our nose is actually more than a kind of snorkel that we use for inhaling oxygen. If we are not breathing, we hold our nose closed with a massive sphincter muscle. This, together with an elongated windpipe in the shape of a gooseneck, keeps water from coming through our breathing passages into our lungs. In contrast to every other kind of mammal, including humans, we have no opening between the nasal opening and the oral cavity. This means that under water, we can stretch our mouth wide open without getting water in the air passages. Our nose is formed in a very complicated way, and just imagine that every kind of whale has its own nasal design. While the baleen whales have two nasal openings, the toothed whales have only one. You can tell by our spout whether it's a baleen or a toothed whale. The spout is either divided into two streams, or only a cloud can be identified. In your children's books, we are often portrayed with a beautiful fountain streaming from the top of our heads. That gives you a false impression, because our noses are not fire hoses, but breathing organs. What you see when we blow is condensed water vapor, something like when you breathe out into frosty air. When we exhale, the gases are expelled through a small opening with considerable force. This generates a strong pressure increase in the air and when it hits the free outer air, our breath expands (you remember from physics: the more a gas expands, the more it cools). This causes the water vapor to condense into droplets. The cloud of water vapor is just as visible in the tropics as it is in waters with icebergs, and the spout is different for each kind of whale. For right whales, it is 9 to 13 feet (3 to 4 m) high, for fin whales 13 to over 19 feet (4 to 6 m), for blue whales over 19 feet (6 m), and for me, 16.5 to 26 feet (5 to 8 m) high. Rorqual whales form a pear-shaped spout. I blow at an angle to the front. You'd be quite right in saying, "To each his own"!

## OUR EAR — A STEREO-SEISMOGRAPH

For a long time, your scientists thought we were deaf. Even though anatomists found hints of a complicated inner ear and highly specialized auditory nerves, these prejudices remained. The rule seemed to be: under water there is nothing to say, so there isn't anything to hear, either. It was said that our ears were just rudimentary leftovers from some hypothetical evolutionary ancestry. Fortunately, in the last few years, your researchers have carried out a lot of experiments, and have completely changed their minds, at least on this. Some have now even suggested that we must be descended from cows, since we have multiple stomachs. Don't let yourself be fooled by evolution theories. Just like you, we are one of God's brilliant ideas. That's why it is so important for me to tell you everything about us in such detail.

Let me get on with it, and tell you about how our ears are constructed.

Even the best transmitting facilities for both sonar signals and our tuneful songs — the humpback whale will tell you about these melodious concerts in a moment — won't produce a masterpiece of communication or pinpoint targeting if the reception facilities aren't just as good. Our ear forms this receiver and it exhibits special details that no other mammal boasts of. Many land animals have gigantic spoon or funnel-shaped ears so that they can receive sounds from various directions. Such protruding external ear muscles are a problem in the water, as they would ruin our perfectly streamlined form. Any one of your divers can tell you that directional hearing under water is exceptionally difficult. For example, a diver can barely tell from which direction a motorboat is approaching. On land, your brain computes the direction of a sound by comparing the minute differences between the time a sound is received by nerves in one of your ears, and the other. This doesn't work in the water, because the sound penetrates your skull pretty much unhindered. Since your ears are attached to your skull, the vibrations arrive at the ear at virtually the same time, and the differences between the time of reception for different directions is hardly discernable.

The Creator gave us an ingenious system which has no equal in the animal kingdom. It provides us with excellent stereo reception, even under water. We have a "high tech" hi-fi system which is free of interference for directional hearing. One noticeable thing about our ear is that it is separated from the bony structure of the skull. The ear's bones are only fastened to the skull by membranes, so they are free to move independently, and sound waves received by the bony structure of the skull are not passed on to the ear. The entire system is reminiscent of a sensitive seismograph, the instrument your geologists use to measure earthquakes. The minute bones of the inner ear — hammer, anvil, and stirrup — have a completely different form with us. Toothed whales use very high frequencies for echo-locating. An eardrum wouldn't work effectively at such high frequencies. That's why some whales have no eardrum at all, and with the others, their eardrum is completely different from that of the human ear. Baleen whales don't need echo-location gear at all, so they communicate in very low frequency ranges (50 Hz or less). Such low frequencies have the advantage that they transmit for long distances in water, so two whales can communicate clearly over distances of up to 62 miles (100 km). That would be the same as two people trying to hold a conversation between Washington and Baltimore (or London and Oxford), without using a telephone. I know what you're thinking. You want to know what kind of messages we transmit on these frequencies that the Creator allocated for us. I'll let the humpback whale talk about that, since he has composed a number of concert pieces in his time.

## THE HUMPBACK WHALE — MASTER SINGER OF THE OCEANS

*Composing and Performing without Piano or Music:* Unlike fish, we happen to be gifted with wonderful voices. With the exception of your talented musicians and birds, we are the only creatures on earth whom God has gifted musically. Our songs don't just vary a certain fixed melody. They are just as varied as the pieces of Beethoven or the Beatles. Our music consists of recurring phrases. When we compose, we obey more than a dozen rules of composition. Each year, we release a new "hit." In the expanses of the ocean, we can effortlessly make ourselves heard over distances of up to 62 miles (100 km). Since our songs are the most interesting and moving sounds to be heard in the seas, U.S. researchers have recorded them in stereo with underwater microphones. A selection of our songs has even been released by a music firm on an LP. We humpback whales are also known for our exceptional hunting methods.

*Clever Fishing:* We use a very refined method. We swim in rising spirals around a swarm of krill, and expel a precisely measured stream of air through the nose. This forms a curtain of tiny air bubbles which act as a net. The tiny organisms flee from the air screen and gather in the center of the cylinder. The circle of air bubbles scarcely reaches the surface of the water, before I swoop up through the center of it with my jaws wide open. With my giant mouth, nothing gets away. Before I swallow, the excess water pours out the sides of my mouth through the baleen. My prey remains stuck in the mesh of this great filtering apparatus. In this way, I filter my nourishment from the sea in hundred pound batches.

*Baleen — The Gigantic Krill Sieve.* All the other baleen whales have similar fish traps. We are the only creature in the entire animal kingdom that has anything like a baleen. Our baleen consists of 270 to 400 plates with a flat triangular cross-section. These are arrayed in the upper jaw and are made of a horn-like material. The lower edge is as fine as a bird's feather. The right whales have an especially large baleen array. Their heads comprise 30% of their total body length. Driving this mammoth fish net through the seas, right whales extract their nourishment from the water like skimming cream from milk. The 350 or so baleens of the Greenland right whale are as long as 14.8 feet (4.5 m). A whale is able to harvest about a ton of krill from 10,000 cubic meters of ocean water.

Now I must introduce you to another relative, who wins the gold medal in any swimming marathon. Read for yourself what motivates him to these long distance achievements.

## GREY WHALE — THE "MIGRATING BIRDS"
### OF THE OCEANS

We grey whales hold the absolute long distance record for all mammals — and we do it by swimming. We do the same thing the migrating birds do, an annual 6,214 mile (10,000 km) journey from the northern Arctic Ocean, through the Bering Straits, to the Aleutians, down the Pacific Coast of America, till we reach the Mexican peninsula of Baja California. Precisely at Christmas time we reach the California city of San Diego. We don't fly in "V" formation like the Golden Plover, but as a group of 40 or so animals, we form an impressive grey whale armada, that navigates unerringly 115 miles (185 km) per day to our goal.

Why is it that we take such a long journey, traveling 12,400 miles (20,000 km), counting the return trip? Just think, that's half the length of the equator, or as far as you would drive your car in a year! You think we travel down south because there's more food there at that time of year? No, not at all. Actually, the opposite is the case. We can hardly find anything edible there. As a matter of fact, we end up eating next to nothing for a period of six months. The only reason we go through all this is for the sake of our children. Our babies are born at the end of January, and we have to be in the quiet lagoons at San Ignacio on the coast of Baja California. Now you understand why almost all of us grey whales have the same birthday. Even though our babies are 14.8 feet (4.5 m) long at birth, and weigh 1.5 tons, they have almost no fat layer at all, nothing to protect them against the cold of the northern Arctic waters. Our young drink 53 gallons (200 l) of milk and gain 44 pounds (20 kg) per day. Our babies drink this extremely nutritious milk for eight long months. For two months, our children are trained in the Baja nursery to be capable long-distance swimmers, so that they are fit enough to make the long return trip to the far north. This all takes place while the mother is fasting. Even the fathers come along, and fast, during this long trip. We need them along, for one thing, because they protect us from the attacks of Killer whales. The other reason is that it's there in the Gulf of California that we have our short mating season. When we return to the arctic, you can understand that we have nothing on our minds but food. When we get back, we feast on krill by the ton, and once again build up a thick layer of fat. This "blubber" layer can be more than a foot thick. We need this blubber not just for insulation from the cold, but also as an energy reserve during our next long foodless trip south.

## Did We Whales Evolve, or Were We Especially Created?

Many of your scientists believe that we are former land animals that returned to the water. If you have paid attention, you have seen that we are formed in such extraordinary ways, and have such special capabilities, that no land animal is remotely like us. Just think about

- our birth in the breech position
- our nursing procedure under water
- our special organs for deep diving
- our ability to compose music
- our ear construction
- our special nose
- our filter apparatus
  our long foodless migration

Evolution for us is impossible. A half-baked diving apparatus wouldn't do us any good at all. Unless we had a complete filtration system, we would starve to death. If we were born head first, rather than tail first, there simply wouldn't be any whales.

As far as I'm concerned — and I truly believe it — I have a great and ingenious Creator who masterfully made me: "Many, O LORD my God, are your wonderful works which you have done; and your thoughts" (Ps. 40:5; NKJV). I explained earlier that we are a sign of the resurrection of Christ. Now I'd like to tell you that we are also related to the Lord Jesus in a completely different way. Just read the beginning of the Gospel of John:

In the beginning was the Word, and the Word was with God, and the Word was God. The same was in the beginning with God. All things were made by him; and without him was not anything made that was made (John 1:1–3).

If absolutely nothing is excepted from the creative work of Jesus, then we whales aren't excepted either. Jesus Christ is not just your Creator, but ours as well.

# CHAPTER 3

# A FOX THAT LAYS EGGS?

## The Platypus

What do you think of a fox with its tail between its legs and pressed against its belly, that brings grass and mud into its den to make a deep nest, and lays eggs? Or what do you think of a fox that spends hours each day on the bed of a stream, diving for food, with its eyes, nose, and ears closed tightly, but still finds plenty of food? You find the whole idea absurd? I don't.

Actually, I'm not a fox at all, even though my pelt isn't any less beautiful or soft than a fox's pelt. I'm not quite the same size as a fox. I'm only 20 inches (0.5 m) from my head to the tip of my tail. I dig my own den, but mine is usually in the bank of a stream. I sleep there most of the day. Only seldom do I slip out into the sun, where I carefully comb out my fur with my hind claws. You see, I only vaguely resemble the fox.

## An Original Crossbreed

It so happens, however, that I'm quite similar to many other animals. (If you want to deduct from these similarities that I'm related to them, then that's up to you!) My tail resembles that of a beaver. The "poison fangs" on the hind paws of my mate could be those of a viper. The webbing between my toes could be from a frog, and my bill could be from a duck. That last item, by the way, is one of my most important organs — and not just for feeding. This bill gave me my name: platypus. I lay eggs like a bird, but nurse my young like a cat. I can swim like a fish, and dig like a mole.

## No Place in the Family Tree

Yes, you're right! If you look at me, I can be a little confusing. Where do I really belong? To the fishes or birds, to the mammals or to the snakes? Actually, I have something from each of these. Many scientists figure that I am a 150-million-year old transition form between reptiles and mammals, an animal that isn't quite complete. I'm pretty modern for my age, don't you think? The scientists who have worked on me have been surprised by my super-modern equipment and my superlative capabilities. They can't explain why such an "old" organism has these capabilities, and are not quite sure on which branch of the family tree they ought to hang me. I don't think much of all that stuff. I don't belong in any family tree whatsoever, but consider myself as a master work of a fantastic artist: God. I know that I am not His only remarkable creation. You yourself are just as much a creature made by His hand.

## UNKNOWN IN EUROPE

Until the 19th century, we were completely unknown in Europe. As the first reports of us filtered in, scientists didn't know whether or not to believe in the existence of such a strange thing. They were afraid of falling for a hoax, and so they decided that somebody had painstakingly fastened a leather bill and webbed feet onto the torso of a beaver. We really do exist. We come from eastern Australia, and are completely at home in the streams and lagoons there where we can find fresh water.

I do admit, though, that I made it difficult for the researchers. Whoever wanted to see me had to follow me into the water at night. I fished there in the darkness, with my eyes tightly closed. If he did happen to see me, he noticed that I can easily swim around any obstacle, and that I chase shrimps and invertebrate animals, and then stuff them into my cheek pouches. Then, above the surface, he could observe how I surfaced with full cheek pouches, gradually emptied the contents into my mouth, and ate at leisure. In this way, I can eat up to half my body weight in food every day. Can you imagine how much food I have to find every single day?

## A FASCINATING BILL

Finally, one of the researchers had the idea of studying my bill more carefully. He found that the soft upper surface of my bill is pierced with thousands of tiny holes. My Creator installed a miniature valve plug in each of these openings, coupled to a sensitive nerve. In this way, the sense of touch is transmitted immediately to the brain, and I can react more strongly than I could to an impulse from my eyes, ears, or other parts of my body. If I had only these mechanical receptors (scientists call them touch sensors), I would have to collide with an obstacle under water before I could react. But that's not the way it works. The researchers went to great lengths to track down the Creator's secret.

Between the touch sensors on my bill, my wonderful Creator distributed a multitude of similar structures, which react to electrical impulse. These sensors are dependent on certain glands that secrete a slimy substance, and therefore only function under water. In addition, there are special nerve endings which also react to weak electrical currents.

Do you really believe that such refinement is the result of chance and necessity, mutation and selection, or whatever other clever words you might use? These words suggest that these things just happened by themselves. From what I have seen, chance doesn't bring anything important into existence. The results of mutation are almost always harmful to the organism. Selection chooses only from things that are already present. It never produces anything new.

While swimming, I swing my bill from side to side two or three times per second. In this way I receive the finest electrical impulses emanated by crabs and other small animals, and thus am able to take off after them.

## A THERMAL DIVING SUIT

Another of my remarkable specialties is the capability to regulate my body temperature. Even in the winter I need to eat, and have to spend hours in the icy water. No other animal could stand the low temperature for so long. My Creator, however, furnished me with a hairy diving suit which insulates me from cold better than the fur of a polar bear. I can also alter my rate of metabolism significantly, so that even after several hours in icy water at a temperature of about 0 degrees Celsius, my body temperature is still 32 degrees.

## A DANGEROUS POISON

Every male platypus received a hollow spur on his hind foot from the Creator. It is up to a little more than half an inch (1 ½ cm) long, and contains a strong poison. There is no other animal in the entire mammal kingdom with such a venom injector. The poison is produced in a gland on the thigh. Your scientists still don't really know why it is there. My partner uses the inward-facing sharp spur during fights against other males of our species, to defend our territory.

The poison is very strong. A dog which is wounded by the spur dies within a short space of time by paralysis of breathing and cardiac functions. I heard of one scientist who tested a small dose, just 0.05 milliliter, on himself (1 ml = 1 cubic centimeter). He injected the poison into his lower arm and later complained of excruciating pain.

## My Tail and Feet

Just as the Creator gave the camel his humps, He gave me a flat tail. As a fat storage system, it is an excellent fuel tank. It also acts as a rudder for me when I swim or dive. When I'm on land, I can press it between my legs against my stomach and can carry all sorts of useful things around with it.

Swim webbing is nothing unusual, of course. Lots of other land animals and birds have it, but it is somewhat refined in my case: on land, webbing is not very useful. As a matter of fact, it gets in the way and interferes with running. I can fold my webbing away inside and so use my feet easily for running, climbing, and digging. I generally try to build my dwelling in the steep bank of a stream. I make the entrances so tight that entering my den presses the water out of my coat. You have to admit: a practical set-up.

## Laying Eggs and Nursing Young

When mating season comes, my mate takes my tail very gently in his bill, and we then swim in tandem in a circle for several days. This is our mating ritual. During that time, several 4-millimeter size eggs migrate down my left egg tubes. There they are fertilized by sperm cells from my mate, and they develop a first soft shell for protection. The eggs (there are three at the most) then migrate into my uterus, where they receive a second shell. When they have reached a size of 12 millimeters (about ½ inch), they get a third and final coating. My young are nourished by these amazing shells during their first days — without an umbilical cord.

There is no additional opening for my offspring to emerge through. The two or three eggs are expelled through the opening that otherwise is used for excretion. That's another reason why the threefold protection is necessary. The sticky eggs land on my belly, and I press my warm tail over them. I incubate my young there until they are ready to hatch.

In the meantime, the Creator causes a single, small eyetooth to grow on the upper gum of my offspring's mouths, with which they are able to tear open the soft, rubbery shell. My tail remains wrapped around them and holds them firmly to my belly. Two days later, I am able to provide them with milk. But you have to understand, I have no breast nipples. The milk simply exudes from a milk-field through my fur. There, my young slurp it up with their soft little bills.

By the way, my milk has an amazing iron content (60 times higher than cow milk). The Creator set it up that way since He knew that the livers of my young are too small to store all the iron they need.

You can see from everything I have said that I'm not a prehistoric animal, an animal that time forgot. My Creator equipped me perfectly for the life I lead on the east coast of Australia, the place I call home.

# CHAPTER 4

# GOD'S LITTLE ROOMMATE

## *The Swallow*

My father came back with a tasty mouthful in his beak. Like a moustache, the food hung out the left and right sides of his mouth. Right away, I opened my beak as wide as I could, but he was not interested in filling my mouth with food. Greedily, I lunged over the edge of the exit hole to grab the rest of the food. He suddenly jumped back, and I fell out screaming. For a split second, I tried to grab him with my feet. I hurtled downward, flapping my wings desperately. Just before the crash I expected, I noticed that I could fly! Reeling awkwardly, I followed my father to the closest tree. After I had rested for a while, I plucked up the courage to jump off on my own. I flew directly after my father, making all the curves and banks, zooms and dives, that he did. Later, I tried to get back into the nest, but it wasn't easy. I managed when father helped me, and I crept back into the nest, which was stuck to the wall, quite exhausted.

## My Name

I am a swallow, more accurately known as *delichon urbica*. In contrast to my relative the smoke swallow, my underside is immaculately white. My tail also differs from hers. I think it's much more beautiful, without those long, silly points, don't you agree? I also think it makes more sense to fasten my nest on the outside of a building, instead of living with animals in a stall. My Latin name shows that scientists are only human, too. Actually, it comes from the Greek *he chelidon*, which simply means "the swallow." Somebody mixed up the letters from *chelidon* and got *delichon*, which really doesn't make any sense at all. Since I live near humans, I was given the designation *urbica*, that is, belonging to a city.

## My Flight Muscles

Do you have any idea why we birds are able to fly? It is not as easy as you might think. Our entire organism had to be specially designed for flight by our Creator. It's not enough just to have feathers. We can move our wings up and down without effort. Most four-legged animals, on the contrary, move one foot forward, then another. You do the same thing with your arms, without thinking about it, when you walk. Of course, it's a small thing, but without this instinctive moving of both sides at once, I couldn't fly a single foot. Furthermore, we have to move our "forefeet" (i.e., our wings) back and forth faster than any other animal. The record is held by our smallest colleague, the tiny, 1.2 inch (3 cm) tall hummingbird. He is able to flap his wings 80 times per second. If you had the same ratio of strength to weight that he has, you would be able to throw 56 sacks of cement higher than 40 inches (1 m) into the air — every second. So you see, flying requires a lot of strength. That means our flight muscles — in relation to our body weight — are among the strongest muscles in the animal kingdom. They make up one-third of our body weight.

Scientists have discovered that an eagle produces a constant energy equivalent of one-tenth of a kilowatt. I admit that I can't do that. I am a lot smaller. Just think what the energy-producing capacity of a human is. It's no more than that of the average eagle. With such a pitiful energy capacity, you wouldn't be able to handle even gliding for one minute, let alone any kind of powered flight.

## MY FEATHERS

You may find them quite ordinary, but look at your own skin with the few hairs on it. Look at the pelt of a guinea pig, the scales of a carp, or the cold skin of a frog — none of these outdo our feathers in terms of complexity, lightness, and beauty. You have undoubtedly heard of the theory which says that our feathers have developed from reptile scales. Well, I can't believe such a thing. I believe what your own confession of faith says: "I believe that God created me, as well as all other creatures."

Just take one of our feathers in your hand, put it under a strong magnifying glass, or better yet, a microscope, and look at the structure. You will find an ingenious combination of strength, elasticity, and lightness ("as light as a feather") that simply can't be imitated, even by your airplane designers.

From each side of the quill in my feathers, several hundred parallel branches reach out. A crane's feather has about 650 of these branches. You could see these with your naked eye, and even count them, if you had to. From each of these 650 branches, another several hundred pairs of "rays" radiate out, both upward and downward. There are, in total, more than one and one-half million of them.

To keep the air from ineffectually streaming through these branches extending from each side of the quill, I need a special device to fasten the hundreds of feather branches together and yet keep them elastic. My Creator arranged this by giving me a special kind of zip. On the underside of each little branch piece, there are hundreds of rounded, and twisted loops. In the feather of a crane, there are 600 of these distal barbules. On exactly the opposite side of the next branch down, there are 600 little hooks, which fit into these loops exactly. The miracle of it all is that the hooks in the loops can slide back and forth, enabling the feather to broaden or to contract again. That's important for me when it comes to soaring. If this little zip device comes open, I can easily put it back together with my beak. Don't I have a wonderful Creator!

## MY WINGS

When air passes over an airfoil, forces arise which push it upward. There's a fairly complicated theory behind that, but I don't want to bore you with it. The striking thing is that I can change the shape of my wing. I do it by erecting an extension of feathers on the front edge of my wing when I need to. This increases the lift. Naturally, this only happens when I am airborne. If the feathers were rigidly anchored to my wings, I could, of course, point them downward and thus obtain some lift, but then I'd nosedive because I would then have to lift my wing upward, and this, in turn, would drive me downward. My Creator took account of this and made sure that my feathers automatically twist somewhat whenever I lift my wings, so that they open like the slats of a Venetian blind, and the air can flow through. When I point my wings downward, they close again, and I can soar high into the air. Since my wings also twist like an airplane propeller each time I beat them, they also propel me forward.

## MY FLYING EXPERTISE

You know that the Creator made us to be excellent fliers. Many ornithologists have even suggested that we spend the entire night in the air, since we don't come back to our nests during the night. Actually, we do spend the largest part of our lives in the air. We zip from place to place like arrows. If our lives are endangered, we fly upward so fast that even falcons are left behind. In order to be able to adjust our flight speed to different situations, we have been given the ability to enlarge or reduce the load-bearing surfaces of our wings.

The Creator used a fabulous mechanism to further perfect the properties of our feathers. There are certain nerve paths in our skin near the roots of our feather quills. If the feathers are excessively loaded by the air stream, these nerves report the fact immediately to our brain. The brain, in turn, immediately gives orders for the individual position of the feathers to be altered. This all takes place in a fraction of a second. More than 1,200 tiny muscles are fastened to the roots of my feathers, to make the mechanism work. Can you still really believe that my feathers evolved from reptile scales?

## My Lungs

If you ever climb the stairs of a church tower, you quickly get "out of breath." You breathe much faster than normal. Of course, with us it's a little different. At rest, I breathe something like 26 times a minute. While flying, it goes up to 490! You can well imagine that a normal lung system wouldn't be able to handle the strain. So our Creator figured out something quite unusual for us.

When I fly, my lungs are supported by a whole row of bellows. These are air sacks of various sizes that are not only connected to my lungs, but also to certain hollow areas in my bones. The constant contraction and relaxation of my flight muscles cause these air sacks to be compressed and expanded at the same rate. They are filled by air pressure coming from the slip stream as I fly. Through this special construction, my lungs are ventilated twice each time I breathe (by inhalation, and expansion of the air sacks). In addition, these air sacks serve as a cooling system for my highly stressed muscle system, and as padding for my inner organs. All of this is absolutely necessary, otherwise, our organs would be thrown to and fro by our constant acceleration and braking maneuvers, and we would simply break apart.

## My Nourishment

I find most of my nourishment in the air. When I'm providing food for my young, I spend at least 15 hours in the air every day. Since we have such slender pointed wings, we are extremely agile, and we can catch insects right in the air. We eat flies and mosquitoes, but also leaf lice and butterflies — whatever is available. While we are eating, we can open our beaks very wide. A few thousand of us in Hungary were able to completely clear a cornfield of black tree lice in a couple of days. Since you don't have so many insects flying around in winter, we have to move to other locations in the south. We fly to the Near East or even deep into Africa. South of the Sahara, we find plenty of nourishment. In April or May, we gladly fly back to our old nest.

## My Trouble

While we're away, sparrows often make themselves at home in our nests. Just imagine, if you came home from your holidays, and some stranger had taken over your home. You'd call the police immediately. Since we don't have any police, we have to drive out the squatters ourselves. You can well imagine that it isn't always particularly pleasant. Sometimes the fighting is so intense that the nest is actually destroyed. One time — I admit, it wasn't a very nice thing to do — we just went ahead and walled the sparrows in and let them starve.

## My Home

I'm sure you have seen my house before. Actually, it is something of a built-on extension to your own houses. I only live there for a couple of months. It's built of a thin mud paste, and is fastened high under the eaves so it's protected from the rain.

Usually, another pair of swallows helps us with the building program, so we're able to complete the nest in 10 to 14 days. Then we help them.

I won't deny that we're very "human" about the whole thing. If our neighbors don't watch out, we steal some of their nesting material, which they have just built into their own nest. That way we save ourselves a lot of flying, but we often pay for it in terms of aggravation. Naturally, our neighbors do the same thing to us.

We build our nest so that it is almost completely closed. Only a small hole remains open at the top. Inside, we carefully upholster with moss, blades of grass, small feathers, and fluff. You can be assured, we always keep the place clean and neat. If it ever looks untidy, you can blame it on the sparrows who have trespassed and made it their own nest.

By the way, do you know that we too appear in the Bible? In Psalm 84, verses 3 and 4, it says:

> "Even the sparrow has found a home, and the swallow a nest for herself, where she may have her young — a place near your altar, O LORD Almighty, my King and my God. Blessed are those who dwell in your house; they are ever praising you" (NIV).

Actually, our ancestors even fastened their nests on the buildings of the temple in Jerusalem. There, close to God, they felt right at home. I know that God is everywhere. That means He is near you, too. I am so happy to have such a wonderful Creator! From my whole heart, I want to praise Him, just as it says in Psalm 84:2: "My heart and my flesh cry out for the living God" (NIV).

Do you feel at home with God, too?

# CHAPTER 5

# COMPETING WITH GENERAL ELECTRIC

## *The Glowworm*

**O**uch! You're hurting me! Please don't pinch my wings so tight. You can hold me in your hand, but just don't crush me! Please remember to set me free. If you like, I'll tell you something special. Okay?

It wasn't hard for you to catch me this June evening, was it? In the dark, you can easily see all of us flying. During the day, you wouldn't notice us at all. You don't find us interesting during the day, do you! Yes, I know, it's our light that you find so fascinating. If you'll just turn me over carefully, you can see the two greenish yellow light spots on my underside. That's the reason you only see our light when we fly overhead. Can you turn me right-side-up again, please? Ouch! Be careful! I'm no more than about one-third of an inch (10 mm) long. You have to be very careful with your big, clumsy fingers, if you don't want to squash the living daylights out of me!

Now turn on your light, and look me over. By the way, if you were in South America right now and laid my relative, the cucuju, in your hand right next to me, you wouldn't need your light. The cucuju's light is so bright that you would be able to inspect both of us without any additional light at all. That's the reason why lots of people there catch cucujus and keep them in little cages, to be used as lanterns.

## UNATTAINABLE LIGHT EFFICIENCY

It's true that I am just a little unattractive beetle, but still, I'm a miracle direct from God's workshop. "Glow worm" *(lampris and Phausis)* or "small St. John worm" are our man-made names. Actually, they are misleading names, as I'm not a worm, and I don't glow. I actually generate "cold" light. That means, in my process of generating so-called bioluminescence, no heat is generated at all. That's really the astounding accomplishment that your engineers have not yet been able to match. One of your normal incandescent lamps transforms only a maximum of 4% of the input energy into light. Even a fluorescent lamp turns only 10% of the input energy into light. The rest is wasted in heat. You have to admit — your lamps are more like ovens than lights. For me, the Creator achieved the greatest possible efficiency in transforming energy into light — that is, 100% of input energy is converted. You really can't do better than that.

Now look at my neck shell. It protects my head better than the crash helmet your motorcyclists wear. Besides that, my Creator formed the hard material in such a way that it is transparent in front of my eyes, and nowhere else. That means I can look out on the world through this window.

If you could please turn off your "oven," I can show you the rest better in the dark. Do you see all the little points of light over in the grass? Those are our little females. They can't fly. At mating time, they creep out on the blades of grass. As soon as a male approaches them, the female stretches her tail, with her light organ, up into the air. That makes the greenish yellow light visible, and the male comes to mate.

Included among my relatives — and I have more than 2,000 different kinds of relatives — is the so-called Black Light Beetle (*photinus pyralis*). In his family, the males and females communicate by means of flashes of light. One of these flashes lasts only 6 hundredths of a second. What is remarkable is that the male sends these flashes at an exact interval of 5.7 seconds. The females answer in exactly the same rhythm, but 2.1 seconds later. So far, nobody really knows exactly why they turn the light on and off so quickly.

In the summer, my mate lays the eggs on a damp spot under a leaf. At first, half-grown larvae develop from the eggs. They spend the entire winter on the same spot and then, in the spring, emerge from cocoons as adult glowworms.

The frogs are among our enemies. If one of them eats too many of us at once — and this does happen from time to time, unfortunately — then even the frog begins to glow in the dark. That must look funny to them! This is because even our eggs give off a little light, as do, of course, the larvae and pupa, too.

What enables us to give off light? I guess you'd be interested to know? In 1887, the Frenchman Raphael DuBois found, in the luminescent mucus of the boring mussel (*Lithophaga*), the two substances that are absolutely necessary for producing light. If these react with each other, light is produced. The Frenchman called one substance luciferin and the other luciferase. The chemical composition of the second substance remains a mystery. Even today, it is only known that it consists of about 1,000 amino acid units. That means that its structure is highly complicated and extremely difficult to figure out. I can only marvel at what great effort the Creator put into us tiny creatures. In studying the other substance, the luciferin, American scientists recently discovered that the number of oxidized luciferin molecules exactly matches the number of transmitted light bursts. This is a confirmation of just how energy is transformed completely into light. Oh, I see you're getting bored, but the matter really is much more complicated than I can explain to you.

## A SHUTTER FOR A LIGHT SWITCH

By the way, let me tell you something else that you almost certainly don't know anything about. Have you ever heard of the lantern fish *(Photoblepharon palpebratus Steinitzi)*? You haven't, have you? It's true we are not related, but he also produces light. Actually, he doesn't generate the light himself, but he obtains it from luminescent bacteria, whose light is produced by a similar chemical reaction to the one that produces my light. An individual bacterium is so small that its light can't be seen. Only a colony of millions produces light strong enough for you to see. The bacteria sit on an oval-shaped light organ underneath the eye. At this location they are nourished with energy and oxygen through a densely branched network of the fish's tiniest blood vessels. Besides this, the Creator installed a kind of shutter for the lantern fish, a black eye fold, that the fish can drop down and in this way "turn off" the light. If he wants to, the fish can send out blinked light signals. The Creator's ideas are boundless. He "lets there be light" in the most varied ways.

## FLASHING TREES

I even have relatives in South Asia. They're quite fond of gathering together in the thousands in trees by the river bank, where they all blink in unison. Travelers in Burma or Thailand haven't been able to find adequate words to express the overwhelming impression this evokes. Sometimes, many of these trees are clumped together; then it's not unusual for each leaf to have a lightning bug on it. You can just imagine how the trees flash. Science has not yet been able to figure out why they all flash at the same time. Maybe the Creator just wants you humans to marvel at His fantasy?!

## REFLECTOR PRINCIPLE

Back to me once again — and then please let me fly away. I still have to tell you about the wonderful light organ with which the Creator equipped me and my friends with. Basically, it consists of three layers of cells. The lowest layer is formed with cells whose plasma is filled with tiny little edged crystals. These crystals act as a reflecting wall — something like the reflectors on a bicycle. The middle layer consists of the actual light cells. They are filled with round particles, the mitochondria, which function as miniature power plants responsible for providing energy. These light cells are equipped very richly with the finest nerves and respiration tubules. The third and outer layer is the skin. At this part of my body, the skin is transparent, so that I can shine my light on humans and animals.

## MINIATURE RAILWAY

I admit that my appearance is not as impressive as the Brazilian railroad worm *(Phrixothrix)*. This beetle larva has two orange lights that "glow" on its front end. If it spots danger, then it turns on a row of 11 green lanterns on its right and left sides, so that it looks like a small train in the darkness.

I don't look like a train. Ladies don't put me in their hair either, as they do with my South American cousin, the speed beetles *(Elateridae)*. Those beetles glow in the dark like diamonds. As for me, I can only blink and my light is only one color. But I still praise my Creator for making me such a small miracle. You, too, ought to join in and praise the Creator.

Now, if you wouldn't mind letting me go first.

# CHAPTER 6

# AEROBATIC EXCELLENCE

## *The Dragonfly*

We dragonflies *(odonata)* are among the most striking forms of insects. In the bright sunlight, we fly, hunt, court, we pair, and lay eggs. We live out our lives before your very eyes. It's probably our spectacular flying that amazes you the most. In fact, I can name nine distinct types of flight which we have completely mastered: neutral flight, cargo flight, patrol flight, menacing flight, mating flight, commuter flight, wave flight, hover flight — as well as many varieties of backward flight.

Among the 800,000 kinds of insects, we are the only true acrobatic fliers. For hours at a time during warm summer days, we drift back and forth over a pond, hardly moving our wings at all. If we see an edible insect, we seize it instantly with a lightning fast movement. If an annoying rival arrives on the scene, we spiral into the air and circle him until he flies away. Even in swamps, we are able to fly through the dense vegetation with elegance and style, without ever bumping our sensitive wings against anything. As you already know, we rule the air near water. We move around like silent helicopters. Even though we beat our wings at a frequency of 30 cycles per second, we make no sound that you can hear. Our wings don't just serve for flying. They also play an important role in the competition for mates. We use them for balancing on precarious perches. We even use them to absorb warmth from the sun, and the tongues of aggressive frogs encounter them as sharp defensive weapons. But still, flying is and remains their chief purpose.

Of our 4,500 different varieties, 80 are present in Central Europe. We are divided into two groups: large dragonflies *(Anisoptera)* and small dragonflies *(Zygoptera)*. Of the many different names, I'll just mention a few, so that you'll get an idea of how varied our family is.

> **Small Dragonflies:** white-legged damsel-fly, *Coenagrionidae* (for example the scarce *Ischnura*), the green lestes, the *Calopterygidae*.

> **Large Dragonflies:** hawkers, (for example, the southern hawker, Emperor dragonfly), the dragonfly, *cordulegastearidae*, emeralds (for example, the brilliant emerald), and *libellulidae* (for example black-likened ortetrum, black-tailed hawkers, vagrant sympetrum, vagrant darter).

Most of the medium-sized dragonflies belong to the first classification of small dragonflies. The larger ones are in the second group. Size is not the most important element in our classification, because some of the smallest of the large dragonflies like the vagrant sympetrum — are just over an inch (3 cm) long, and the largest of the small dragonflies — the *calopterygidae* — is almost two inches (5 cm) long. It is much easier to classify us by our wings. When they rest, the small dragonflies fold their similar-sized front and back wings together. The large dragonflies spread their different-sized wings out from their bodies. In flight, too, there are essential differences: the small dragonflies move their front and back wings at different rates, while the large dragonflies' nervous system synchronizes their wing movements. For now, I'm only going to talk about the large dragonflies. The German poet and zoologist Hermann Löns (1866–1914) was so impressed by the Emperor dragonfly that he wrote:

> None of the other chalcolestes viridis comes close; it is more beautiful and swifter than the large anisoptera. Its wings are formed of gold filigree, emerald green jewelry adorns its head, and its body wears finery of black-traced azure blue silk.

*Aerodynamic Body:* Like all insects, our body consists of three segments: head, thorax, and abdomen (Figure 1). Our

Figure 1: The basic body structure of a dragonfly.

construction includes numerous special features that are especially adapted for our lifestyle, and particularly for our ways of flying. Our matchstick long, thin abdomen, which looks like a balancing stick, is remarkable. It actually stabilizes our flight, and conceals our digestive and reproductive systems. Our segmented construction and the connecting skin provide high elasticity and good maneuverability. Every individual segment consists of hard breast plates and strong backing, just like an ancient knight's armor. Our Creator used chitin for our external skeleton. This special material is extremely light, and is hardened by calcium deposits. Thanks to this two-component system, we have a skeleton that combines extreme strength, with minimal weight. Thus a Horseshoe Blue dragonfly weighs only one-fortieth of a gram. That means you would need 80 of these small dragonflies to match the weight of a single one-cent piece.

## Legs for Catching Instead of Walking

We rarely use our thin and remarkably thorny legs for walking, but they are very important when we are flying. Normally, we tuck them in close to our bodies when we are flying, to minimize air resistance. If we see prey, we spread our six legs out in front of us to form an opened "catcher," so that we can "fish" our snack out of the air. Our in-flight menu consists of ephemera, mosquitoes, and moths. Since we can only spot our prey at close range, we only have a fraction of a second to complete the flight maneuver and actually catch the target. Our eyesight, our nervous system's ability to react, and our flight technique are stretched to the limit by the high targeting accuracy required to catch our prey.

## Our Flight Equipment — Forerunner of Your Helicopter

We have completely different principles for flying from any other insects. The Creator developed a special kind of equipment for us, and I'd like to tell you about it now. Most insects fly by a so-called "teapot" principle. Just imagine a pot with a lid that is a little bit too small, and two spoons which have been placed under the edges of the lid. If you push the lid down, the spoons rise up. If you lift the lid, the spoons drop. In most insects, this pressure is supplied by muscles that are found in the thorax area, which are connected to the "lid" and to the "bottom of the pot." With every muscle contraction, the body tightens up and this raises the wings. The opposite motion occurs when the muscles are relaxed. In contrast, our flight motor operates on a fundamentally different principle.

Our strong flying muscles are connected directly to the wing joints by tendons. The Creator made these tendons out of a material called *resilin*, which has extraordinary mechanical properties. Unlike any other material, it is completely elastic, and can therefore store a huge amount of energy which can be released at the necessary moment. Picture a flattened plastic bottle which springs back to its original shape immediately after being squashed. Together, the wings and the resilin form a similar system to that of the bottle, and have a particular oscillating frequency.

Our Creator designed us with so many of the intricacies of flight built in that we are well able to take care of ourselves once airborne. We were simply made to fly. Your aeronautical engineers have a way of describing flight characteristics in terms of the so-called *Reynolds number*. It characterizes the relationship between the viscosity of the surrounding air, and the speed and size of a flying object. For large birds, this air coefficient is of little or no importance, but it's a different story for insects. Actually, for small insects, the viscosity of the air is such an important factor that they really tend to swim through what is for them "thick" air. Insects with a small Reynolds factor must beat their wings much faster than larger insects, just to make headway. It turns out that our Creator gave us a very favorable Reynolds coefficient. We can easily reach speeds of 25 mph (40 km/h) without constantly having to beat our wings. Even when flying slowly, enough lifting force is generated by the air streaming over our wings to keep us aloft.

*Forehead anemometer:* In addition to an effective flight propellant, speed control is necessary for optimal flight. The Creator installed two antennae on the front of our heads, at the optimal position for measuring air flow. In flight, these feelers are bent back by the air in the slipstream. Sensory cells in the base of the antennae transmit the measured values to the brain, where the data is used to calculate speed in relation to the environment. For flight precision as well as style, these measuring antennae are one apparatus I simply couldn't do without.

*Wing membranes thinner than paper:* The combined weight of our four wings is a mere five thousandths of a gram. This wafer-thin, transparent flight apparatus is a masterpiece of lightweight construction technology. If you were to imagine our wing membranes forming the material of a large surface, then a square meter (10.8 square feet) would weigh only three grams. The cellophane you use for wrapping, made of polyester or polyamide has to weigh three to four times as much to have the same strength. Our wings are reinforced by veins — your aeronautical engineers would call them "spars." The diameter of these tubes is only 1/10th of a millimeter, and the thickness of the walls of the tubes is only 1/100th of a millimeter. These hollow tubes serve not only for bracing the wing, but are also the transport lines for the blood fluid (hemolymphes), and the data cables of the nervous system, as well as the system for oxygen supply and carbon dioxide removal.

*Calculated Security:* If you have come to the conclusion that the Creator skimped on safety by saving on materials, then please permit me to put the record straight.

All living creatures are provided with safety reserves just as they are in your technology, so that premature breaks and failures do not occur. For example, you could withstand the weight of 17 men on your thigh bone. You need this reserve for running or jumping, in order to withstand greater stress. In the mouse, the thigh bone is able to withstand a load of up to 750 times the usual. After all, they have to be able to jump from a kitchen cabinet without breaking a leg. The same goes for wings. A chaffinch, for example, has a total wing surface of about 23 square inches (150 square cm), for a body weight of just under an ounce (25 g). That means that 1.5 square inches (10 square cm) of wing surface support 1.7 grams of body weight. The 2.3 square inches (15 square cm) that we dragonflies have support a mere 0.5 grams, i.e., 0.33 grams is supported by 1.5 square inches (10 square cm). This corresponds to a security margin that is five times greater than that of the chaffinch. You wouldn't have expected that now, would you?

*Wing pattern as personal identification:* Our wings are glass-like membranes, reinforced by many branches of a network of circulation tubes. The longest arteries give cross-sectional stability, while the many small branching arteries, and the clearly visible "wing marks" *(pterostigma)* provide longitudinal stability. A glance at the wing pattern of the blue-green Southern Hawker and that of the *Mecistogaster lucretia*, reveals that the Creator used distinctly different construction principles to achieve the same purpose: irregular polygons and regular rectangles provide the necessary wing stiffness in each case. Dragonflies with a higher wing beat rate, like the blue-green Southern Hawker (30 beats per second) need to have narrow reinforcements. Other kinds with a lower wing beat rate can get by with simple, but unbelievably precise, right-angle lattice pattern. An example of this is the *Mecistogaster Lucretia* with its long, thin wings, beating 15 times per second. The membrane cell construction technology makes the wings ultra-light, but still very stable. Plus, if you have an eye for design, you can tell our different varieties apart just by examining the varying arrangement of the lengthwise and transverse wing arteries. The significance of the reinforced edge cells on our wings was only recently discovered by the Swedish scientist Ake Norberg. The species dependent variation in cell thickness toward the tips of the wings also has an important aerodynamic function.

In high speed diving and gliding flight, they prevent so-called wing flutter.

*Turning flight:* For turning flight, we utilize a special technique which again differentiates us from other insects. Split seconds before a turn, we twist our body on its long axis. Viewed from the front, the thorax and abdomen are no longer lined up horizontally, but are displaced. A different angle of attack is then created for our inside wings which enables us to make elegant curves. Other insects — beetles in particular — utilize a different principle: the wing on the inside of the turn beats in a smaller angle. In this way, the thrust on that side is reduced, and the desired turning motion takes place even with the same wing beat rate.

## NO HONEYMOON FLIGHT WITHOUT PREVIOUS CODE CHECK

You have already heard about some of our most remarkable characteristics, but if I were to tell you about our mating habits, you would certainly think that these are not just unusual, but really quite original. Since we are designed for flight from head to toe, we think it is totally natural to mate in mid-air. That's got your attention! I'm sure you're now thinking about the many constructional details that would be necessary for something like that. You probably think that the flight maneuvers alone would be impossible. Actually, the Creator didn't run out of ideas and, even here, He came up with something special for us. Just listen. Before the wedding, the male's courting flight takes place. This mating flight is marked by rapid wing movements around the cross-axis, whereby the wings beat alternately. To the approaching female, this appears as a thin blue side band. Needless to say, this is not unattractive to her. In the forward flight phase, the front wings beat with a reduced angle of frontal attack. They provide the lift to remain aloft. The back wings beat at a high angle of attack to the rear, and thus achieve maximum propulsion. For split seconds, conditions are reversed. Now the rear wings take over propulsion. In backwards flight — our flight specialty — everything works in reverse. The steeply angled front wings produce the necessary force to make backward flight possible. The back wings are adjusted almost horizontally, and provide the necessary lift.

The male now flies to the female from above, and seizes her on the head with the so-called abdominal hook (in the case of small dragonflies, the female is seized by both the head and the first thorax segment). This big semicircular "tong like" apparatus sits at the very end of the long abdomen, and serves to anchor the two insects firmly together during mating. In the middle, between the hooks, are a pair of short appendages which vary from type to type. These fit into a matching system in the female, in a "key-lock" arrangement. This ingenious code system ensures that only the same types of dragonflies mate with each other. After this secure grip is established by the identifying code system, the partners form the "mating chain" in tandem flight, male in front female to the rear.

This peculiar wedding is necessary because of another unusual part of dragonfly construction. All dragonflies carry their sex organs at the end of the abdomen. How can the male sperm get to the female? The solution of this riddle lies in an ingenious idea: the male sex organ has two functions. The sperm is produced at the end of the body, and then is transported to the "appropriate place" into a sperm pocket. Depending on the type of dragonfly, this happens either before or after the two unite. The male bends the rear of his abdomen into the sperm capsule of the secondary copulation organ, and thus fills it.

Now the female bends the rear of her abdomen down and forward so far that her sex opening at the end of her abdomen reaches to the sperm-filled holder on the second and third abdomen segment of the male. In this way, the mating chain is altered to form the "mating heart" or the "mating wheel." After the successful transfer of sperm, the mating wheel is released.

Now in tandem flight, the pair fly to the place where the eggs are laid. In this, the leading male directs the way to an appropriate egg-laying location. In the case of meadow dragonflies, the landing takes place on alder or willow branches that hang over the water surface of a pond. Now the most difficult part begins for the female: 200 eggs must be deposited under a hard bark surface. Do you have any idea how this can be done? A tiny saw on the laying borer of the female serves as an effective tool. The sawing action, which deposits tiny particles of dust in the water, takes just a few seconds. Then the long eggs are laid in the moist cells of the bark. During this long procedure, which can last up to four hours, the male appears to be idle. He is, in fact, protecting the neck region of the female with his legs, keeping her free from other males eager to mate, who lost out in the mating competition.

You may well ask, "Why bother with such an unusual mating method?" Well, for us, everything has to be arranged for absolute flight-worthiness. So we take to the heights of the air even during mating. In this sense, you could consider our independently movable front and rear wings as special equipment. In hovering flight, we are even able to move our wings against each other. Because of our flight technology, we need our lengthy abdomen as a balancing beam. Especially during the complicated maneuvers of mating, we need to be able to stay absolutely motionless in the air. The pinpoint coupling, even in turbulent air, requires unparalleled flight precision.

Did you know that the pioneer of your helicopter technology, Igor Sikorsky (born in 1889 in Kiev, died in 1972 in the USA), got the idea for the development of the helicopter from his dragonfly observations? The four adjustable rotor blades enable both forward and backward flight, just as our four wings do. In spite of the well-known technical capacity of your flying machines, the capabilities of your helicopters and of ourselves, are worlds apart. Our flight is a hundred times more nimble, and absolutely silent. A gentle rustle indicates our flight when our wings touch, but it all takes place with an unmatched degree of efficiency.

## OUR REMARKABLE EYES

Whoever wants to maneuver fast and gracefully has to have user-friendly navigation instruments. So, we have our ball-shaped, knitting-needle-head-sized eyes. Among all the insects, we are the real "eye animals," because our seeing apparatus composes the majority of our head surface area. The high degree of curvature creates an extremely wide field of vision.

Our eyes are composed of up to 30,000 six-sided individual facets. Each of these facets forms a distinct eye with its own tiny lens. This gives each eye an individual angle of vision. All of them together cover a very broad field of vision, without any individual eye, or the head, having to move. Our eyes are much more capable than yours in many ways. We are able to perceive 200 blinks of light per second, while you can only perceive one-tenth of that. If there was television for dragonflies, a film intended for us would have to be transmitted at ten times the speed of your TV stations.

Let me talk about some of the physical principles involved here. In contrast to your eyes, the image arising from up to 30,000 individual eyes is actually quite imperfect and unclear. While each of our eyes contains only eight vision cells, you have 78 million. So you have an image that is scanned much more finely. This implies that our visual acuity is only a fraction of yours. Nevertheless, we have a wonderful imaging system, full of the Creator's technical refinement, that substantially increases the quantity of the given visual information. Rapid sequential bursts of light, up to 200 per second, are individually registered as separate events. Our movements are almost exclusively flight movements, whereby we perceive the environment as being in constant motion. In flight — and again, that is our primary activity — the optical center receives substantially more information than when we are at rest. Our "flight" visual acuity is thus substantially greater than you would expect from the anatomical construction alone. Our vision is approximately the same as that of your TV cameras: the light beam with which the image is sampled is comparable to the function of each individual eye. The beam alone is unsuitable for picking up the smallest detail of the form of an image, but if you move the beam and display the variations in brightness that arise by sampling the image in sequential impulses, one can obtain a detailed image of the observed object. So your TV and my compound eye generate an image in much the same way: both systems use a combination of highly developed fast processing power, together with low resolution optical imaging equipment.

## OUR COLORED DRESS

Even if you have gotten to know our insect species fairly well, I dare not neglect one characteristic. It is our impressive coloring! After the butterflies, we take the second place in the competition for beauty and color. With us, you can find every color imaginable: from sharp color tones, to metallics, to dark and rich hues. How do all these nuances and color compositions come about? I won't explain these colors scientifically, otherwise I would have to delve into the sophisticated knowledge of chemistry, as well as going back to physics, but there are three independent principles which you should know.

1. *Pigmentation: Why are Chinese people yellow, Indians red, and Africans black?* Well, there are certain color substances, pigments, in their skin which are characteristic for these races. This is exactly the method the Creator used to color certain types of emeralds, for example the vagrant darter, as well as some of the smaller dragonflies. In contrast to your races, our chemical bonds produce a substantially stronger color effect, as for example, *melanin* for yellow, red, brown, and black, *ommine* for violet brown, and *ommatine* for red-brown tones. In the same way, white, yellow, or reddish *pterines* are used. You can well imagine that the appropriate mixtures of these coloring agents permits a rich display of color.

2. *Structural Colors:* With this method, the colors are not produced by organic molecules, but by means of a physical trick. The color impression comes by means of light diffraction of the rays of sunlight falling on thin, platelet-like layers of chitin armor. All metallic shimmering dragonflies are actually colorless, but still, they glisten in richly colored splendor. Such structural colors are seen, for example, in the blue-metallic *calopterygidai*, the green to copperish green lestes, and the shining green Brilliant Emerald. The *Coenagrionidae* and *Aeshnidae* dragonflies, with their enamel-like green and blue, also have additional dark bodies in their chitin armor causing light dispersion, which enhances the multiplicity of colors even more.

3. *Wax Colors:* This method is reminiscent of the coating seen on ripe plums. The bluish ripening of the abdomen on the common green lestes comes from a wax coating that is produced by skin pores. The color arises by diffuse reflection of the sunlight.

What is the purpose of all these colors? The various kinds of color patterns make it easier for us to recognize various species, and also makes it easier for us to find a mate. Coloration can also serve as a good camouflage. As we are animals with varying body temperatures, coloration helps us to warm up in the mornings. In the same way, our colors give us appropriate protection from ultraviolet radiation, and regulate the force of sun radiation we receive. Still, all these effects could have been achieved with a much lower number of colors. The astonishing variety must have another reason: it is the Creator's richness of invention, and His love for beauty. The Lord Jesus said:

> See how the lilies of the field grow. . . . I tell you
> that not even Solomon in all his splendour was dressed
> like one of these (Matt. 6:28–29; NIV).

We come from the same Creator's workshop. So you shouldn't be surprised at our beauty and glorious color.

# CHAPTER 7

# AN APPARENTLY SIMPLE ORGAN — BUT ACTUALLY, A PRIME EXAMPLE OF INGENIOUS DESIGN AND CONSTRUCTION

## *The Human Eye*

How shall I introduce myself? I'll do it with a riddle:

I look at you, but you don't see me.

You carry me with you, but you don't notice me.

All people need me, but they don't feel me.

My very existence is a miracle, but many don't know it.

Who am I? Haven't you guessed yet? Well, let me add a little to my description: I have a spherical shape, and I am completely transparent. My diameter is no bigger than one-third of an inch

(9 mm), and I'm only 4 millimeters thick. My volume is tiny, only 0.06 cubic centimeters. Just imagine! I'm 30 times smaller than a ripe cherry. Oh, and something else: without me, you couldn't see a thing.

I've almost given myself away: I'm one of the most important organs of your visual apparatus — the lens of your eye. Before I begin to tell you about myself, I want to say something about sense organs in general. Precisely here you can perceive some of the principles of the work of my Creator. Keep that in mind, and you will understand my own biography much better.

## THE WORK OF THE CREATOR AND THE LAWS OF NATURE

*Sense Organs:* If you examine the world of sense organs from a technical perspective, you will never get over a sense of wonder. You find such ingenious and technically refined designs that you find nowhere else. If these inventions were all created by humans, I can tell you that you would need a special patent office just for dealing with the patents for sense organs alone. These are all God's ideas, and no technical authority is in charge of registering these ideas. The Psalmist was thinking of the richness of these ideas in creation when he prayed, "O LORD, how great are thy works! and thy thoughts are very deep!" (Ps. 92:5). You ought to know how God works. In every instance of design and construction, in the entire range of living creatures, never does a design principle violate a natural law. Or, to put it another way, to achieve their goals, the varied organs utilize the physical and chemical laws in what are often the most ingenious ways, but in ways which are often difficult to understand.

Many different measuring procedures are used in your technology and in natural science, each having a high degree of accuracy. You accomplish the most accurate measurement of time by the use of atomic clocks, but precision can even get a great deal better, since the limits of the laws of physics are far from being reached. The so-called "relative uncertainty" is a standard for the uncertainty of a measurement. One can use a meter stick to measure the length of a meter with an uncertainty of 0.5 mm. The relative uncertainty is thus 0.5 mm/1000 mm = $0.5 \times 10^{-3}$.

Present levels of relative uncertainty in atomic clocks are at a level of about $10^{-13}$, and according to the Heisenberg Uncertainty Principle, this level could be reduced to $10^{-16}$. So up until now, no measuring process has been developed for which the precision and utilization concept has approached the limits of what is physically possible. The Creator has realized such amazing concepts again and again precisely in the field of sensory organs, achieving the limits of what is technically and physically possible.

I want to explain another important fact. Please differentiate clearly between how that which the Creator made works and His creative work. While all created things and all processes in nature are subject to the laws of nature, the creative actions of the Creator himself cannot be explained in terms of those laws, because they themselves are a result of creation. They are not its cause.

Now I want to tell you more about the visual organ, because I am an irreplaceable part of that organ. That's true not only for humans, but for all seeing animals. Just imagine, each dragonfly eye consists of thousands of individual compound eyes. Each individual eye is equipped with half a million switching elements. Each of these functional elements is a hundred times smaller than the smallest switching element in your modern computer technology. Naturally, each individual eye has its own lens, or, more accurately, microlens.

## Do You Know How Your Eye Functions?

Even your own eye will never cease to amaze you. For every image which you see, an optical image of 130 million individual cells is processed. In cooperation with still unknown processes in the nervous system, a high definition image of the thing you are observing is generated in your brain. These highly complicated processes are largely beyond the understanding of your scientists.

Just imagine you had to use semispherical shaped film, instead of the conventional flat form, in your camera! The images on that film would be as distorted as the ones you see on the distorted mirrors at the fair. That is just the kind of world that arises on your retina at first.

The Creator has installed fast-running programs in your brain which instantly correct distortions in the image, so that the world around you appears as a flawless image, just like a photograph. The sense of vision, along with the brain, does something quite wonderful: Your sense of vision is not intended for measuring physical objects precisely. Rather, it is constructed to meet biological requirements. That means that at varying distances, you don't judge the size of the object by the size of its image on the retina. Rather, the size which you assign to a distant object is different from its corresponding size on the retina. You are familiar with representing things in perspective: the sense of vision reports its findings to you in terms of converging lines — not the physically "correct," but rather the biologically significant values. For the correct evaluation of the environment, the estimation of the size of an object is necessary, no matter what distance it may be from the viewer. The evaluation program in the brain processes the physical data received by the sensory organs: it enlarges, reduces, and adjusts them precisely, so that the information is presented in a way that makes sense biologically.

To put it another way: it is the brain which turns the eye into an apparatus which is much superior to a pure instrument of physics. It is able to see in the darkest shadows as well as in the brightest sunlight by automatically adjusting the optical range of operation. It can see colors. It can perceive white paper as being white, even when it is illuminated by bright light of varying colors. It contains the ability to perceive colors in essentially the same way, whether in the dim light of early morning, or in the bright light of midday. Color and shape are perceived as the same, whether the object is close or far away, and even if the lighting varies radically. One fundamental capability of the visual system (and also of the hearing system) is the ability to recognize and remember objects, situations, other organisms, and humans. This ability still functions even when you haven't seen people for a long time. In a class reunion, you recognize former classmates in spite of changes brought about by the many years which have passed. The important thing to remember is that the sense of vision has a kind of precision which cannot adequately be described in terms of physical measurements alone.

You know Aristotle's famous saying, "The whole is greater than the sum of the parts," which of course applies to all living things. If complexity, structure, purpose, and inventiveness are recognizable on the level of the individual elements of an organ, how much more so at the level of the organ as a whole. So instead of talking about the eye as a whole, I want to concentrate on myself for a bit, on the lens, a tiny detail of your eye.

## A Manufacturing Impossibility

I'd like to clarify some points regarding my technical capabilities. See if you can follow my train of thought. Just imagine you wanted to get a company that makes precision optical components to introduce me as one of their production line products. How do you suppose you would go about it? Now, you would quite correctly say that the company would need a catalogue of specifications in order to make the lens. Well, no one knows me better than myself and so I've prepared a list of just six of the most important points for you.

*Concept for the lens:* In your conventional optical industry, the camera focusing is made possible by either shifting the lens system, or the film position. The eye needs a lens system which consists of just one lens, which still meets all the possible requirements. In order to meet all of these conditions, it would be good to get away from the photographic industry's restricted principle of hard, non-flexible lenses and use a flexible "glass body" instead. All necessary focal lengths between 1.5 and 2.75 inches (40 and 70 mm) and focus settings should be catered by means of lens deformation. The lens should be elastic and supple enough to change its form easily. A system of push and pull mechanisms at the lens edges should be responsible for changing its shape. A command center (brain) needs to be developed in order to coordinate the extent to which the shape of the lens should be altered. When each element works in harmony with all the others, then the lens should be assured of acquiring the optimal form which is in accordance with the given conditions.

*Material Synthesis:* A pumped circulation system is to be used as a source of raw materials and to provide for the removal of processing wastes. This should resemble a watery solution (blood) containing various dissolved substances. The lens's own production system is to be connected to this general supply network. The necessary materials (proteins) are to be produced on site, by chemical means, ensuring that no temperature exceeding 98.6°F (37°C) may occur. Which of the millions of possible proteins are necessary for the lens development is a matter which can be easily ascertained. The materials should be named and coded to the given code system. The process of chemical synthesis must be indicated and the management of the process engineering is to be undertaken.

*Production Process:* The production system should be computerized and fully automatic, requiring no manual intervention. This computer system is to contain all the production programs and is to perform the process control supervision of all chemical and energetic reactions. To ensure a steady process, expended materials are to be replaced continuously. This should in no way disturb routine operation. Breakdowns and down time must therefore be kept to an absolute minimum. Because of this grand conception, individual lenses cannot be mass produced and then singularly finished. Each one must be produced according to the individual given conditions, based on a computer-controlled construction plan.

*Optical Characteristics:* Although proteins are not generally transparent, a method must be found of producing a lens with a very high light transmission co-efficiency. The refractive index, which determines the refraction of light in various media should remain constant throughout the lens. The various methods employed to overcome the many construction problems encountered should in no way interfere with the incoming light.

*Miniaturization:* Because of the essential decentralized construction of the lens elements, which must be maintained for years and years, a cellular construction technique is to be used. Every cell is not only to carry out its optical functions, but is also to be an independent and fully functional production unit. An extreme level of miniaturization is to be used to fit the fabrication process complete with energy generation and data processing systems into 0.00366 cubic inches (60 cubic mm). I realize that your computer systems are well known for their high-density memory chips. However, for this purpose they simply don't come up to scratch and will have to be replaced by a more space-saving technology.

*Reliability:* Finally, the lens operation must have a lifetime warranty. That means what it says, generally from 70 to 80 years, and up to 100 and beyond in certain cases.

## The Creator's Solution

Do you see what I'm getting at? Nobody could meet these requirements. There isn't an optical, chemical, precision mechanical, or analytical instrument company in the world that could meet these specifications. All of your brilliant Technological Institutes for Advancement, which consider themselves "high tech," wouldn't even come close to fulfilling them. Yet these are the tasks I carry out day by day, for your benefit, although you take them for granted. Let me do my best to present the Creator's solution.

*1. Transparency:* A very special mixture of two different types of proteins is used in my construction. The lens, with a protein content of 35%, has the highest protein concentration of any body organ. Two completely different proteins are used to create the correct optical characteristics — crystalline and albumin. The former is well known for its water solubility. These proteins are unique. They are not found anywhere else in the body. The transparency is achieved through the reciprocal interaction of the two proteins in the presence of water. The biochemical balance is carefully controlled to maintain transparency. This requires a complicated, though automated, system that is based on finely tuned control principles. Should an imbalance occur, say through excessive water concentration, or through a change in the concentration of protein molecules, then the transparency may be adversely affected. This biotechnical control process, like all technical processes, requires energy. The Creator took care of this by building tiny generators into the lens, which take energy from the biochemical process itself. Your coal-fired generation stations may have a high working temperature, but their efficiency leaves a lot to be desired. As for my generators, they produce 100% of their energy from the chemical energy of their surroundings. Keep in mind that this all happens at very moderate temperature, pressure, and concentration of reactants. To achieve this, the Creator developed a system whereby a substance with very special characteristics controls the reactions under the required conditions. Your chemical engineers call these substances catalysts. Two of my 100 protein molecules achieve just that and are known as enzymes.

*2. Internal Structure:* Other deciding factors in the achievement of the lens' characteristics are its form, organization, and internal structure (Figure 2). It's only when you magnify my image that you begin to see the highly specialized and tightly packed order of protein layers. Looking at these layers, I'm always reminded of the orderly stacked layers of planks in a mill (Figure 3). The lens cells bind together tightly but still manage to keep the lens

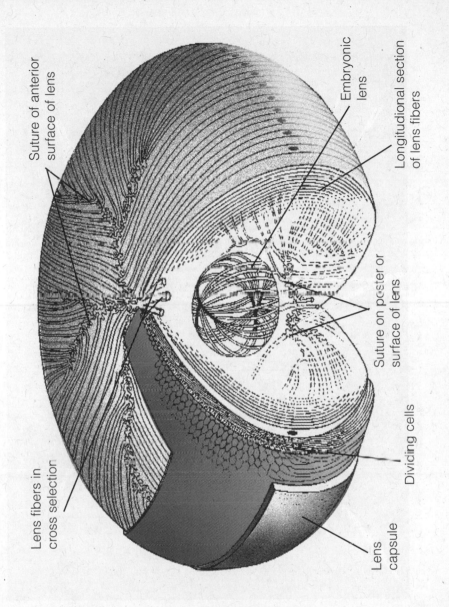

Suture of anterior surface of lens

Embryonic lens

Longitudional section of lens fibers

Suture on poster or surface of lens

Lens fibers in cross selection

Dividing cells

Lens capsule

Figure 2: Cross-sectional view of the human eye. The core in the middle (so-called embryonic lens) has a Y-knot on both its front and rear poles. Cells that are joined to the hub of the Y-knot are connected to the fork of the Y-knot of the opposite pole. The lens is surrounded by a thick transparent elastic capsule (membrane).

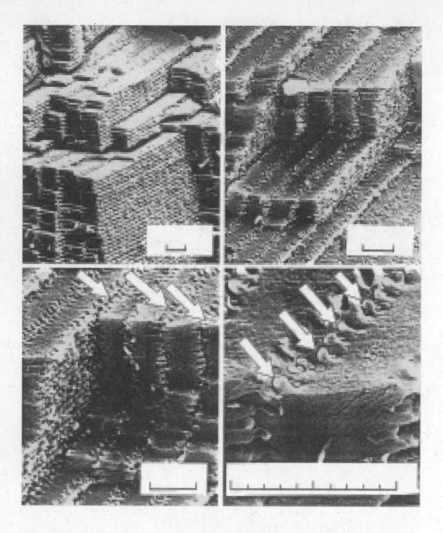

Figure 3: Microscopic eye lens structure. The four different levels of magnification shown by the raster electron microscope display the precisely ordered layer structure. The length of one-hundredth of a millimeter has been drawn to scale for each picture. The protein layers are knitted together to form an elastic compound with the aid of peculiarly formed ball joints (marked with arrows on the two lower diagrams). This allows setting of the focal length by means of adjusting the shape of the lens.

flexible. Each individual layer is fitted with an original hooking mechanism which resembles clasped hands. Precisely this packaging method is necessary to guarantee the high degree of transparency. The correctly ordered layering system, together with the mesh system and the wonderfully constructed ball and socket joints, absolutely amaze your process engineers. The Creator didn't choose the seam separation haphazardly either. It has been finely matched to the wavelength of visible light, so that deformations are negligible.

The wafer-thin protein layers and the elastic clasping mechanism have another important purpose: the lens's shape can be easily modified. In its relaxed state, the lens is quite flat and focuses on distant objects. Sinewy fibers which emanate from a circular cilium muscle achieve this by keeping the lens taught. For close-up focus, the muscle flexes together which in turn relaxes the holding fibers letting the lens, with the aid of its inbuilt elasticity, to return to its more rounded shape. This ingenious and well-thought-out ordering of the layers in an elliptical shape allows every geometrical shape corresponding to the required refractive index (focal length) to be formed, depending on the applied force.

*3. Production Process:* The processes used in my production are extremely complex, and only the external effects may be observed. Just how this fully automated manufacturing system comes to convert all of the raw materials into the end products and organize them all into the correct form remains, even to today's scientists, largely unknown. The recorded information in the DNA-molecule nevertheless plays a central role as far as the control of the growth processes is concerned.

## MY ORIGINS

You've just been looking at a small building block of the eye in terms of its complexity, ingenious construction, and the wonderful variety of ideas which back it up. Nevertheless, this describes the eye about as well as a brick could describe Buckingham

Palace or a screw could describe a car! To explain the existence of the eye in the context of a selection process was acknowledged to be impossible by none other than Charles Darwin. He wrote about the subject in his book *Origin of Species:*

> To suppose that the eye with all its inimitable con-trivances for adjusting the focus to different distances, for admitting different amounts of light, and for the correction of spherical and chromatic aberration, could have been formed by natural selection, seems, I freely confess, absurd in the highest degree.

Every individual part of the eye can only enable sight in the presence of all other parts at the same time and provided they are all working together correctly. If the eye were complete except for the lens, the whole organ would be useless. Evolution can neither design nor plan ahead. Even existing products can't be modified. Otherwise, the evolving universe would have to have been like a building site with the notice: "Works temporarily shut due to renovation."

As all of mankind's attempts to answer the question of his origin somehow miss the point, I trust the Bible's God of creation, who has kept us well informed.

"Who gives him sight. . . ? Is it not I, the LORD?" (Exod. 4:11). The Psalmist also shows God to be the builder and archi-tect of the eye: "He who formed the ear, shall he not hear? He who formed the eye, shall he not see?" (Ps. 94:9; NKJV).

# CHAPTER 8

# ONE IN 150,000

## *The Earthworm*

So, you don't think much of me? Well, listen here! Ultimately, like you, I'm just one of the Creator's originals. Now please don't look down on me. I was created just as perfectly as you were, although I've been given other duties. That's why my Creator also had me take on another form. Besides, I'm more important to you than you think!

If you will have a little patience and listen, you'll certainly be amazed, and may even learn to respect me and my kind.

## MY UPBRINGING

My first memories are of a rubbery abdominal bandage, sealed at both ends, where I safely grew. I left it behind though, as soon as I felt strong enough. My real home is in the soil where you plant your tomatoes and cucumbers, play football, and build homes. That's where I dig till I drop. My home is fairly deep — about 5 feet (1.5 m) under the surface. That puts me deeper than the average worm. As far as I know, the deepest recorded depth for a worm is about 26 feet (8 m). I'm homeward bound twice yearly; winter and summer. That's when I curl up cozily, and wait for better times.

## MY NAME

I'm your everyday garden worm or earthworm. If you like being really precise, you can also call me *Lumbricus terrestris.* That sounds very scientific, but it generally means the same thing. Sometimes I'm called the common earthworm, but that doesn't say much for my uniqueness as one of God's creatures. I may be common, but nevertheless I'm a wonderful creation.

Some of you have a problem — you see yourselves as ordinary. You think you're unnecessary and even quarrel with God about it. What do you think you're doing! Even the most everyday things have so many wonderful aspects to them that it's hard to stop marveling at them once you've started. Furthermore, God's world can't just consist of remarkable creatures; it needs ordinary ones, too, like you and me!

## MY BURROWING TECHNIQUES

Have you ever thought about how I burrow? Perhaps you wondered how I manage it. After all, I don't use a shovel like you, nor do I use a digger for that matter. I just need to use my strong pointed head. It's so finely formed that it can fit into the smallest crevice. I nose my head into the crack, flex the muscles, which my Creator so amply supplied me with, and force the earth apart, just like a wedge.

You may ask yourself how I get by without a skeleton. My Constructor had to come up with a pretty good idea. If I want to use my muscles correctly, I need a support, as pressure always produces counter-pressure. You've most certainly learned that in physics at some time or another. So my wise Creator fitted me with two pressure pillows that are arranged in each of my many segments (try and count them), around my middle intestine. Scientists have measured that a pressure of 1,560 Pascal (= 1.54% atmospherical pressure) results when I flex my muscles. That may not sound like much to you, but remember, I'm a worm. Let's change the subject; I'm not sure I want to bore you with any more complicated details.

## My Movement

Now you must know this: Have you ever studied how I get about on the ground? I'm sure you've noticed how I can stretch and shrink my segments. What you probably didn't see is that there are "anchors" which I throw out on both sides each time I compress a few segments. I push out two short brushes on each side into the surrounding soil. "Anchored" in this way, I can stretch my frontal segments and thus make good headway.

Please don't get me wrong: these brushes are not the remnants of some primeval fur coat. My ancestors were just as smooth as I am, as they too were specially constructed for our way of life. Anyway, what would I do with a fur coat underground? These anchor brushes don't even disturb me, and when I don't need them, they conveniently hide away in pockets of skin.

Do you think that all this developed by itself? Well, you don't believe that your wristwatch developed and constructed itself, do you? I'm much more complicated than a watch, don't you think? At least, that's my opinion! Can your watch reproduce?

## My Stature

It's about time I said something about myself. I'm now about one year old and 7 or 8 inches (20 cm) long. Some of my family can live to be ten years old. Our largest relatives live in Australia. With a cross-section of over an inch (3 cm), some of them achieve an overall length of 10 feet (3 m). Pretty big for a worm, eh?

My brain resides above my pharynx. Although it's smaller than yours, it works in principally the same way. Perhaps you thought I didn't need one? Would you like to explain how I'm supposed to move in a hurry, with three contraction and expansion waves running simultaneously over my body, without a brain? As for my eye, it's just a light-sensitive area on my head. My Creator knew I wouldn't need anything complex. What use would I have had for anything more complicated? I only need to recognize when I've reached the soil surface and should be digging back into the depths. Sunlight is dangerous, if not deadly, for me. All the same, I can withstand dehydration of up to 70% of my body weight, or alternatively I can live 100 days underwater. How long do you think you'd hold out?

## MY ENEMIES

I really don't like talking about them, but if you want to understand me, you'll have to hear about that, too, because it has to do with one of my most amazing characteristics. My enemies have quite a difficult time trying to kill me, as I can lose parts of my anatomy without it adversely affecting my life! Not only that, but under certain circumstances, I can regenerate missing limbs. My Creator programmed my genes so that my tail grows back if it should accidentally get cut off, but that's not all. Even my head with all its tiny intricacies can re-emerge. I'm not pulling your leg, it's true! Unfortunately, my enemies, the moles, also make good use of this. They usually catch me if I happen to stumble into one of their homes. They first bite off my head, complete with three or four segments. This, in effect, makes escape impossible (you try moving without a brain), and stick me onto a wall in their larder. A Polish biologist once counted 1,200 worms in a chamber like this. If I survive the mole's voracity through the winter, I still have a chance to escape, provided my head has grown back. Unfortunately, the mole is not my only enemy. Well, you know, earthworms are world renowned for their politeness . . . so I won't say any more.

Did you know that we also suffer because of the fall of man? Your ancestors have a lot to answer for. We all are waiting expectantly for the day when the whole of creation will be set free from this "bondage of corruption." If you'd like to read about it, open up your Bible to Romans 8:19–23!

## MY DIET

Now, first and foremost, I have been given work to do in this world. The Creator gave me the job of fertilizing and loosening up the soil, so my pathways run all the way through mother earth. If it gets too hard and I can't find any cracks to squeeze through, then I simply "spit" on the earth in front of me. Then when it's softened up, I just eat it. That's my own special way of getting into the deeper earth layers. I gobble up foliage and other organic materials. Just imagine all the things that wander through my stomach, the remainder of which ends up in little heaps of muck on the surface of the soil! It really isn't that revolting; it turns out to be the best compost on the market.

## MY PERFORMANCE

Scientists have calculated that given 2.5 acres of good soil, one hectare (= 10,000 $m^2$), the worms contained in it can produce more than 220 pounds (100 kg) of humus in a 24-hour period. That's 40 tons a year, spread evenly over the soil surface. Of course, I don't work alone. Besides me, about 150,000 other earthworms live in the space of an average football field. In a rich meadow, there could even be a couple of million of us. You'd definitely run into difficulties if you wanted to weigh all of us. We'd weigh about 1,100 pounds (500 kg) on the scales. That's about as much meat as you would get if you raised beef cattle on the same field.

At any rate, we get a lot of praise from experts for our amazing restructuring and processing performance. If you give us a little time, say 300 to 400 years, you can be sure that the whole earth surface to a depth of about 16 inches (40 cm) has wandered through our intestines.

That's how we complete the job that our Creator gave us. The very fact that we're here, though you may think it insignificant, serves to glorify Him.

# CHAPTER 9

# THE LIVING ELECTRIC MOTOR

## *The Intestinal Bacterium:* Escherichia coli

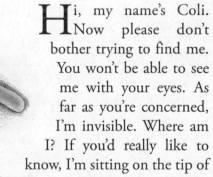

Hi, my name's Coli. Now please don't bother trying to find me. You won't be able to see me with your eyes. As far as you're concerned, I'm invisible. Where am I? If you'd really like to know, I'm sitting on the tip of your supposedly clean index finger.

If three hundred of us were to form a line, then the chain would have a length of 1 millimeter, and if you were looking very closely you might just spot it. If we lined up like this in a thousand rows all next to one another, we would still only take up the space of one square millimeter.

Actually, my full name is really *Coliform bacteria*. Where did I get a name like Coliform? I suppose it's because I spend most of my time in your intestine. Please don't be offended by my home background. You see, together with millions of my kind, I play an important part in your nutrition. In your intestine, I break down all the unusable items in your food so that they can be absorbed by the intestinal walls. I hope you don't mind if I help myself while I'm at it. After all, we do a lot more for you than just that. Provided there are enough of us, we protect you against hostile and sickness-inducing micro-organisms. We are only harmful in tissues outside of the intestine. So be a little more careful with me and don't forget your personal hygiene.

As you can't see me, I'd like to give you a brief description of myself. Please forgive me if I exaggerate a little. Imagine a large loaf of bread with six hefty ropes at one end, which are all at least 6.6 feet (2 m) long. If you take a closer look at these ropes, you'll notice that they all leave the loaf at right angles. Now just imagine the ropes revolving very quickly, at up to 100 r.p.m. That's about twice as fast as the generators that make domestic electricity.

The rope or flagellum, as it's more correctly known, is built up like a round chimney, in which the bricks wind in spirals right up to the top. If you imagine the chimney with a cross-section of 39 inches (1m), then based on this scale it would have to be 3,280 feet (1,000 m) high. The bricks correspond to the molecules in the flagellum. Of course, the molecules are inter-connected much more elastically than the bricks in a chimney. Now imagine that the chimney itself is rotating at breakneck speed. Remember, in reality, my flagellum is at most two hundredths of a millimeter long.

My Creator certainly built the most wonderful and highly integrated things into me. I can live, move about, feed myself, multiply, and be of service to humanity at the same time! Even the makeup of my harmless looking cell wall is extremely complex. Besides the various membranes, there's a layer of proteins, a support skeleton, polysaccharide, a lipid layer, and much more. My DNA chain, where my Creator stored the necessary information, is approximately a thousand times longer than myself. Can you imagine how ingeniously the molecular structure was packaged so that it could fit inside me, not to mention the information density. Did you know that my DNA chain contains about as many characters as are in your Bible?

I can't go into all of my astonishing details right now, but I just have to tell you more about my six rotating electric motors. These are essential to my mobility. Like any electric motor they have a stator, rotor, and the necessary housing. The axle sits vertically on the membrane surface and is built into two neighboring membranes of the cell wall (see Figure 4). The inner membrane forms the non-conducting layer (dielectric) of the capacitor, which is on the outside positively and on the inside negatively charged. A voltage of 0.2 V is generated. Positively charged particles (hydrogen ions) flow inside and thus drive the motor with electric energy. I'm able to run my motors both forward and backward and, with the help of my rotating flagella, I can attain a velocity of 200 microns per second (0.2 mm/s); that's equivalent to swimming my own body length 65 times a second (not including the flagella). If you'd like to compare this with your own swimming pace, it would be the equivalent of jetting through the water at 250 mph (400 km/h).

Some of you think that this ingenious motor came about through mutation and selection, but don't forget, as long as one part remains incomplete, all other "developments" are useless. A rotation motor that can't rotate has no advantages.

There's another thing I'd like to let you in on — my function as a "chemical" taxi! My Creator gave me the ability to actively locate the area of highest food concentration and to subsequently swim there. I also notice when I'm facing waste materials and thus avoid them. That's why I've been fitted with a highly intricate navigation system, which provides my six motors with the necessary control signals. Of course, without a navigation system

Figure 4: *Escherichia coli* – the most commonly known bacteria. The detailed diagram explains how the parts of the motor which rotates the bacterial appendage (lat. flagellum = whip) are arranged.

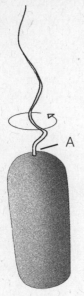

A

Coliform
bacteria

Detail at A

10 nm = 0.000 01 mm

Angle piece

Flagellum

Bearing

Outer
membrane

Peptidoglycan
layer

Inner
membrane

Rotor

my motors would eventually leave me up the creek. A navigation system without a motor is just as useless. What use is it to know where the food is, if you can't get to it?

My navigation system has a parallel in your life. The greatest goal that the Creator has given you is eternal life. What use would it be to you, to know that there is eternal life with God, if you had no possibility of getting there? Be assured, that just as the Creator has given me the motor system to get to my food, He sent you Jesus Christ as the way to the source of life. If you'll believe in Him as your Lord and God, you will receive eternal life.

# CHAPTER 10

# A COMPLETELY INSOLUBLE FUEL PROBLEM

## *The Golden Plover*

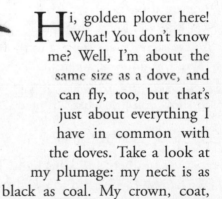

Hi, golden plover here! What! You don't know me? Well, I'm about the same size as a dove, and can fly, too, but that's just about everything I have in common with the doves. Take a look at my plumage: my neck is as black as coal. My crown, coat, and back are all shiny black. Then take a look at how beautifully my Creator framed all of my feathers. See how everything shimmers gold-green on top? I'm not called the golden plover for nothing — *Pluvialis dominica fulva*, as the scientists say. God gave every one of His creatures something special, don't you think?

## A Hollow on Permafrost Soil

I was born in Alaska, although some of my species come from the East Siberian Tundra. These are regions where, even in summer, the ground only thaws on the surface. Only small shrubs, mosses, moorland growth, and lichens can survive. It was up there in the open tundra that I broke open my shell after 26 days of incubation. I found myself, together with my brothers and sisters, in a little hollow upholstered with moss and dry leaves. Our parents fed us, as you might imagine, with vitamins and proteins from fruit and meat in the form of sour redberries, juicy caterpillars, black berries, and crackling good beetles.

We grew quickly, and soon learned to fly. It's so exciting! Walking is a different matter, though. If you saw me, you'd have to laugh. You're absolutely right — I'm really wobbly. My Creator obviously intended to make me this way. Do you seriously think, it could have happened "by accident," or as some call it, a little more pompously, through "material self-organization"?

Did you know that I'm a great fan of the Hawaiian Islands? You're right, that's quite a long way from Alaska! How do I get there? It's quite simple really: I fly. My Creator didn't make me a fast sprinter or swimmer, but He did create an ace flyer! I'd like to show you just what I'm made of.

## 50% Overweight

My brothers and sisters and I were just a few months old. We had hardly learned to fly when our parents left us. They had flown on to Hawaii. We weren't aware of that at the time. To tell you the truth, we didn't really care where they were. In fact, all we could think about was our appetite, and we ate ourselves silly. In a short time I put on 2.5 ounces (70 g) — that's more than half my own body weight. That's something you should try to imagine! Have you any idea what you'd look like if after three months instead of weighing your usual 165 pounds (75 kg) you weighed 254 pounds (115 kg)?

Now, I'm sure you want to know just why I ate so much. Quite simply, my Creator programmed me to. I needed this extra body weight as fuel for the trip from Alaska to Hawaii. That's about 2,500 miles (4,500 km). Yes, that's right, you heard me, 2,500 miles! Not only that, but I can't stop once during the whole trip. Unfortunately, there aren't any islands, rocks, or dry patches on the way and, as you know, I'm a pathetic swimmer.

## A Quarter of a Million Pushups

My friends and I fly for 88 hours — that's three days and four nights — over open water, without a break. Scientists have worked out that we flap our wings about 250,000 times. Imagine doing 250,000 pushups — that would be a reasonable comparison.

Here's another question for you: How did I know that I had to put on that extra weight to get to Hawaii? Who told me to go there anyway and in which direction should I fly? I'd never flown that route before! There aren't any orientation points along the way. How were we supposed to find those tiny islands in the Pacific? If we hadn't found them we would surely have met our end after our food reserves were used up. In that sector, for hundreds of miles, there's nothing but water.

## An Autopilot

Your scientists are still scratching their heads trying to figure out how we get our course and can correct it, even after an inflight storm takes its toll. We fly through fog and rain, whether sunshine, starlight, or overcast skies, and still get there. Even if they do ever dream up a way that could explain how we do it, they won't know how we came to have such astonishing capabilities. I'd like to let you in on it. God, the Lord, gave us a built-in automatic pilot. Your jet aircraft have similar devices. They're hooked up to computers that continuously monitor current position and compare it with the programmed course. They then make the necessary adjustments to lock on target.

Our Creator pre-programmed us with the co-ordinates of the Hawaiian Islands so that we have absolutely no trouble getting there! This complete system is not only reliable, but has also been miniaturized for portability.

Do you still believe that it's all just a coincidence? I don't! Just think for a minute: The original golden plover, whatever that is, decided one day to gain 2.5 ounces of fat. Then suppose he decided to fly off just by accident. Of course, in the same way, he just happened to fly in the right direction and didn't go off course during the complete 2,800-mile journey. Naturally, he then found the right islands in the Pacific.

Then there are the young golden plovers he'd left behind. Would they have been able to have the same good fortune? Just think, the slightest deviation from their programmed course would have been enough, and all would have been hopelessly lost.

## A Precisely Defined Velocity

You know, that's not the whole story. To fly 2,796 miles in 88 hours, I have to cruise at about 32 mph (51 km/h). Scientists have since discovered that that's the optimal speed at which we can fly. If we fly more slowly, we use up a higher proportion of our energy for forward propulsion. If we flew faster, we'd use up too much energy combating friction. It's the same with your car. If you drive faster than 70 mph, you'll use more fuel for the whole trip, because of the extra air resistance involved. Now, you can stop at the next gas station. I can't. I have to get there with 2.5 ounces of extra fat and must contend with occasional headwinds.

## A Computational Example

Are you fond of mathematics? Well, just go and get your calculator. Scientists have found out that golden plovers convert, per flight hour, 0.6% of their body weight into motion and heat. By the way, your flying machines are of a far inferior construction. So, for example, a helicopter needs, in relation to its weight, 7 times and a jet 20 times more fuel than I do.

At take off, I weigh about 200 grams (7 oz); 0.6% of that is 1.2 g. So one hour after departure, I'm down to 198.8 g, 0.6% of that makes 1.19 g. Take that from 198.8 g and you get 197.61 g. That's what I weigh after two hours in flight. Take 0.6% from that and. . . . Well come on! Keep at it — you'll see that mathematics also serves to glorify God.

At the end of my journey, I must weigh at least 130 g; otherwise all of my reserves would have been used up, and I'd crash into the sea and drown. Keep calculating: After the third hour, I'm down to 196.42 g, after the fourth, 195.24 g ... Keep on calculating — I'm waiting. . . .

What's the matter? Oh yes, you're quite right, the calculation doesn't work — 70 g isn't enough in reserve to get there. I'd actually need 82.2 g to make it, as you correctly calculated. After 72 hours, all my fuel would have been exhausted and I'd crash into the sea 500 miles short of Hawaii.

## An Unparalleled Solution

You see, my Creator thought of that, too. He gave each one of us two items of lifesaving information.

1. *Always fly over the great seas in groups, never alone*

— and —

2. *Organize yourselves into a "V-Formation."*

In a formation like this, everybody saves 23% of the energy compared to that used when flying alone. Of course, this isn't the case for the chap at the apex of the formation, but he doesn't stay there all the time. The strong flyers share the load at the front; the weaker ones stay back where it gets progressively easier to fly the farther back you go. In this "cooperation," we are actually practicing biblical teaching, which is better known as the Law of Christ. "Bear ye one another's burdens" (Gal. 6:2). In this way we can reach our winter quarters safely. We even end up having a few grams left over. Our Creator took into account that it is always possible that we could run into headwind. He shows us just how much He cares for us.

Do you still think that I was made by coincidence and that it brought me this far? Not me! I squawk at chance. I'd rather sing my Creator's praises.

# CHAPTER 11

# ANIMALS THAT DID TALK

We called this book *If Animals Could Talk*. Animals are not, according to our general experience, fond of expressing themselves in human language. However there have been some exceptions. The Bible mentions two animals that really did speak to man — in an audible human tongue and with a specific message. The first animal, the snake, was taken over by the devil, and used to entice mankind into disobeying God. The following conversation which took place between the snake and Eve may be found in the Book of Genesis.

Now the snake was the most cunning animal that the Lord God had made. The snake asked the woman, "Did God really tell you not to eat fruit from any tree in the garden?"

"We may eat the fruit of any tree in the garden," the woman answered, "except the tree in the middle of it. God told us not to eat the fruit of that tree or even touch it; if we do, we will die."

The snake replied, "That's not true; you will not die. God said that, because He knows that when you eat it you will be like God and know what is good and what is bad."

The woman saw how beautiful the tree was and how good its fruit would be to eat, and she thought how wonderful it would be to become wise. So she took some of the fruit and ate it. Then she gave some to her husband, and he also ate it (Gen. 3:1–6; Good News Bible, Today's English Version).

God had forbidden Adam and Eve to eat the fruit of the tree of the knowledge of good and evil. They were disobedient and let themselves be enticed into eating it anyway. God knew what that meant; that evil would disrupt the relationship between Him and mankind. They became guilty because they listened to the wrong voice. That's what caused the so called "fall of man," that decisive event in the history of mankind, as a result of which we've all been suffering, right up to the present day. Hopeless, irrevocable? Not at all! (Take a look at the following chapter, *Where from? Where to?*)

The **second animal** which the Bible records as having spoken was Balaam's donkey. Who was Balaam? His abilities as a prophet in Mesopotamia were well known, and the king of Moab, Balak, heard about him. Balak felt threatened by the Israelites, and knew that they would be making their way through the Moabite plains on their way out of Egypt into the Promised Land. He decided to hire Balaam and use his abilities to weaken the Israelites. This was to be achieved by means of a curse.

Balaam set out on his way to Moab to discuss the plan with Balak. On his way, an invisible angel of God blocked his path. His donkey recognized just how dangerous the angel could have been for Balaam. It refused to budge, even under the blows of Balaam's whip, and thus saved Balaam's life. As a miracle, God permitted the donkey to speak. We have a biblical record of the unusual dialogue:

> Then the Lord gave the donkey the power of speech, and it said to Balaam, "What have I done to you? Why have you beaten me these three times?" Balaam answered, "Because you have made a fool of me! If I had a sword I would kill you." The donkey replied, "Am I not the same donkey on which you have ridden all your life? Have I ever treated you like this before?" "No," he answered (Num. 22:28–30; Good News Bible, Today's English Version).

## TWO ANIMALS — TWO VOICES

The animals spoke — something that goes contrary to their natural capabilities, but nevertheless made possible by a higher power. The snake is an instrument of God's adversary; Balaam's donkey a tool in God's hand. Eve and Balaam didn't hear the animal's own voice, but the voice of the one who used it.

There are lots of voices speaking to us today, affecting our thoughts, feelings, and actions. Still, they all fall into one of two categories of forces which show their interest in mankind. One force works toward destruction and evil, the other is the voice of God, who wants to give mankind security and eternal life. Which one is governing your life?

# CHAPTER 12

# WHERE FROM?
# WHERE TO?

Dear Reader! We hope you enjoyed our stories. We would like to take this opportunity to add a few comments to our book. We, an information scientist and a physics graduate, both believe in the living God, the Father of our Lord Jesus Christ.

We want to show, with the aid of these stories, that it's neither boring nor antiquated to believe in God; nor is it necessary to give up your intellect or inquisitiveness. On the contrary, many things become clearer and more sensible when viewed from the Bible's perspective. It can even help to bring about positive results in scientific work.

Everybody confronted by the wonder of life asks himself at sometime or another the inevitable question as to the origin of it. There are only two possible answers to this question.

1. *Life is a coincidence.* It came about through mutation and selection systems. Everything developed "by itself," in stages, over a period of millions of years. Although scientists have discovered that living organisms have many meaningful and highly complicated functions, a reason for all this is denied, as this would presuppose a planner. The biochemist Ernest Kahane put it this way in his *Weltbild der Evolution (World Picture of Evolution):* "It's absurd and complete nonsense to believe that a living cell creates itself; but I believe it, as I can't imagine it happening any other way."

2. *In the beginning, God created the heavens and the earth and all life, and He guarantees its existence.*

If this is true, it has consequences for my life. It means I'm not the product of *Chance and Necessity* (Jacques Monod, 1910–1976), but I am the product of a Creator, who obviously has plans for me. My life has a hope and a goal. It doesn't need to peter out meaninglessly, as Ernest Hemingway (1899–1961) so hopelessly complained: "My life is a dark way, that's leading nowhere."

The all-important question regarding the origin of this world and all life has been answered by God unambiguously and clearly in His Word. In the account of creation, the Bible testifies to the creation of the animal world and of man as described in the Book of Genesis.

Fifth day of creation: creation of the animals of the air and of the seas.

> Then God said, "Let the waters abound with an abundance of living creatures, and let birds fly above the earth across the face of the firmament of the heavens." So God created great sea creatures and every living

creature that moves, with which the waters abounded, according to their kind, and every winged bird according to its kind. And God saw that it was good. And God blessed them, saying, "Be fruitful and multiply, and fill the waters in the seas, and let birds multiply on the earth." So the evening and the morning were the fifth day" (Gen. 1:20–23; NKJV).

Sixth day of creation: creation of land animals and of man.

> Then God said, "Let the earth bring forth the living creature according to its kind: cattle and creeping thing and beast of the earth, each according to its kind"; and it was so. And God made the beast of the earth according to its kind, cattle according to its kind, and everything that creeps on the earth according to its kind. And God saw that it was good. Then God said, "Let Us make man in Our image, according to Our likeness; let them have dominion over the fish of the sea, over the birds of the air, and over the cattle, over all the earth and over every creeping thing that creeps on the earth." So God created man in His own image; in the image of God He created him; male and female He created them. Then God blessed them, and God said to them, "Be fruitful and multiply; fill the earth and subdue it; have dominion over the fish of the sea, over the birds of the air, and over every living thing that moves on the earth" (Gen. 1:24–28; NKJV).

This text shows us beyond doubt that we were created by God, and have even been made in His image. We are a product of His handiwork, and He wanted us. The completed work of creation received His own verdict of "very good."

Today's world is no longer very good. There's suffering and tears, hardship and cruelty, sickness and death. Why did these negative phenomena come to plague us? Although God warned

us about the effects of our disobedience (Gen. 2:17), man mis-
used his gift of freedom, and we came to an incisive event in time
and space, to the "fall of man." From that point onward, the Law
of sin came into effect: "For the wages of sin is death" (Rom.
6:23) — and man came into the firing line. If we stay under this
power of death, then when our earthly lives are over, we'll end
up lost for eternity. God doesn't want that to happen, and so He
prepared a way of escape, which leads to eternal life with God.

## Now for the Good News

God has a wonderful announcement for mankind: "I have
a plan for you! I love you! Please don't avoid Me anymore. I'm
offering you a chance to get to know Me personally, and I'd like
to give you the gift of eternal life."

That's no empty promise. In order for God to make this
offer, He had to sacrifice His Son. He had to give Him over to
ordinary men, who mistreated Him and nailed Him alive to a
wooden cross. Jesus Christ was prepared to make this sacrifice
because He knew that He was the only one who could save us
from eternal condemnation.

## A Righteous God

God is not prepared to tolerate all evils in silence. He doesn't
allow everything to happen without a penalty! Guilt will always
be penalized: "It is appointed unto men once to die, but after
this the judgment" (Heb. 9:27). At this judgment there will be
two sorts of people to be clearly differentiated between: for those
who believe in the Lord Jesus, God sees the penalty for sin as
already paid. For those who ignore Him, it is still due.

The Bible says, "The Lord is not slow in keeping his promise, as some understand slowness. He is patient with you, not
wanting anyone to perish, but everyone to come to repentance"
(2 Pet. 3:9; NIV).

The Bible describes what you have to do to be exempted
from punishment: "Whoever believes in him [Jesus] will not be

disappointed. . . . whoever will call upon the name of the LORD will be saved" (Rom. 10:11–13; NASB). Everybody who turns to Christ in this way is, according to His words, set free from the judgment: "Whoever hears my word and believes in him who sent me has eternal life and will not be condemned; he has crossed over from death [eternal condemnation] to life" (John 5:24; NIV).

## A WORTHWHILE OFFER

We would like to encourage you to do exactly that and accept God's offer. Call on the name of the Lord: that means pray to Jesus Christ. Perhaps you're not quite sure what to pray, perhaps you've never spoken with Him. We'd like to help you with this prayer which you can alter to fit you personally:

> Lord Jesus Christ, I realize that I cannot stand before You and the living God with the sins of my life. You came into this world to save lost sinners. Your death on the cross was the price so that I too could be exempted from punishment. My life is an open book to You. You know of all my failings, every wrong of my heart, and my indifference toward You up to now. Now I ask You: Forgive me all my trespasses, and take away everything which is not righteous. I thank You that You're doing that right now. You are truth personified, and because of that I can rely on the promises in Your Word.
>
> Now Lord, I ask You to fill my life. Lead me along the way which You want to show me through Bible reading and Your leadership in my life. I know that in You I have entrusted myself to the Good Shepherd who only wants good for me. I want to trust You in all areas of my personal life. Give me the strength to make a break from my previous sinful behavior. If I don't always succeed, let me see it as a mishap and confess

it to You then and there. Let me have new habits that have Your blessing. Change my attitude toward You and with the people I come into contact with everyday. Give me an obedient heart and open the Bible to me so that I may understand it correctly. I want to accept You as my Lord and follow You. Amen.

If this prayer really came from your heart, then you have now become a child of God: "To all who received him, to those who believed in his name, he gave the right to become children of God" (John 1:12; NIV). The complete life that God promised you starts with your becoming a child of God. Not only that. The gift of eternal life is yours as well. All heaven celebrates the occasion of your turning to Jesus Christ, for in Luke 15:10 He says: "Likewise, I say unto you, there is joy in the presence of the angels of God over one sinner that repenteth."

We came to God in this way, too, and we'd like to give you a few tips, so that you won't be disappointed at the beginning of your Christian life.

1. Start reading the Bible daily, to get to know the will of God. The Bible is the only book authorized by God. This book provides the necessary nutrition which you'll need for the new life. You can't do better than to start by reading the Gospels. John's Gospel is well suited to the new believer.

2. Talk to God and Jesus Christ daily in prayer. This will provide you with strength, and it will change you. You can include everything — troubles and joys, plans and intentions — in your prayers. Thank the Lord for everything that moves you. A "spiritual circulatory system" comes into being through Bible reading and prayer, which is very important for a healthy spiritual life.

3. Keep in touch with other true believers. If you take a glowing coal out of a fire, it soon dies. Our love for Jesus Christ can grow cold if it's not kept alive through the companionship of other believers. Join a church where the Bible is its foundation, and work with the believers there. A good, lively church where they believe the Bible is an indispensable requirement for life as a believer and for spiritual growth.

4. In your reading of the Bible you'll find lots of helpful advice for all aspects of your life, as well as your relationship with God. Learn to practice everything that you have understood and you will be blessed well and truly. The best way to show your love for the Lord is by obeying Him: "For this is the love of God, that we keep his commandments" (1 John 5:3).

5. Tell others just what Jesus Christ has come to mean to you. Many people have not yet accepted this saving Gospel. They need our example and witness. Now it's your turn to work for God.

We're delighted and rejoice with you that you have genuinely turned to Jesus Christ and become one of God's own.

# THE AUTHORS

**Werner Gitt** was born in Raineck/East Prussia (Germany) in 1937. He studied engineering from 1963 to 1968 at the Technical University in Hannover, Germany, and graduated as Doctor of Engineering at the Technical University in Aachen, Germany, in 1970. Since 1971, he has been supervisor of information technology at the Federal Physics-Technology Institute (Physikalisch-Technische Bundesanstalt, PTB) in Braunschweig, Germany, where he became a director and professor in 1978. He has written numerous scientific papers in the field of information science, numerical mathematics, and control engineering, as well as several popular books, some of which have been translated into Bulgarian, Croatian, Czech, English, Estonian, Finnish, French, Hungarian, Italian, Lithuanian, Kirghizian, Polish, Romanian, and Russian. In 1980, he became a member of the executive committee of the study group "Word and Knowledge." Since 1984, he has been a regular guest lecturer at the State Independent Theological University of Basle, Switzerland, teaching on the subject of "Bible and Science." He has held lectures on related topics at numerous universities at home and abroad and has spoken on faith and science in a number of different countries (including Australia, Austria, Belgium, France, Hungary, Kasakhstan, Kirghisia, Lithuania, Namibia, Norway, Poland, Portugal, Romania, Russia, South Africa, Sweden, Switzerland, and the USA).

**Karl Heinz Vanheiden** was born in Jena, Germany, in 1948. He studied physics from 1968 to 1971 at the University of Halle, Germany, and then was called to Christian youth work in East Germany. Between 1975 and 1991, he taught youth work, homiletics, and prophecy at the Burgstaedt Bible School. From 1985 through to 1990, he was a member of the executive committee of the work group "Faith and Knowledge" in the former German Democratic Republic. Since 1992 he has been touring as an evangelical preacher.

## God's Amazing Creatures and Me!

Helen and Paul Haidle

This intricately detailed book shows pen and ink illustrations of animals and gives a devotional for ages 6 to 10 with each animal. Cleverly demonstrates biblical principles through facets and designs of God's creation.

Children 6-10
96 pages • Spiral-bound
ISBN-13: 978-0-89051-294-4
ISBN-10: 0-89051-294-9
$8.99

*Available in Christian bookstores everywhere!*

## In the Beginning
## Was Information

A Scientist Explains the
Incredible
Design in Nature

Dr. Werner Gitt

Information — it's one of the most fundamental parts of our world, yet we don't often think about it. This classic book, now being published by Master Books, demonstrates the importance of information to life of any kind. More to the point, it demonstrates the necessity of an Organizer and Originator of the information necessary for life.

Dr. Gitt argues that God is not bound by the laws of nature, but instead uses them for His own purposes. He also shows that the highly complex information present in DNA mitigates a non-intelligent beginning for life. He advocates for assurance when dealing with the Bible's information, that this collection of books is not only free of error, but that no useless information is present, as well.

5 3/8 x 8 3/8 • Paperback • 260 pages
ISBN-13: 978-0-89051-461-0
ISBN-10: 0-89051-461-5
$13.99

*Available in Christian bookstores everywhere!*

# MASTER BOOKS®
# SCHOLARSHIP
# ESSAY CONTEST

## $3000
### COLLEGE SCHOLARSHIP

The Master Books® $3000 college scholarship is open to any high school junior or high school senior or the equivalent thereof from any public, private, or homeschool venue. The applicant must be a U.S. citizen and have a minimum GPA of 3.0 or above (on a 4.0 scale). This scholarship is a one-time award and may be used at any accredited two-year, four-year, or trade school within the contiguous United States. This award covers only tuition and university-provided room and board. The scholarship monies will be forwarded to the college, university, or trade school of the winner's choice upon receipt of a copy of the winner's confirmed admission to their chosen school.

Visit www.nlpg.com/scholarship to download your application along with:

 **Essay Topic and Deadlines**

**Rules, Regulations, and Conditions of Eligibility**

Master Books — your Creation Resource Publisher — is a division of New Leaf Publishing Group.